CUBA

BEHIND THE EMBARGO

Jason R. Old

ANTHROTOURISM PRESS

Tampa, Florida, U.S.A

"No hay cosas imposibles, sino hombres incapaces." –
José Martí

Published by
ANTHROTOURISM PRESS
Tampa, Florida 33607
U.S.A.
For more information about this book and **ANTHROTOURISM PRESS,** *visit www.anthrotourist.com*
1st Edition Book design copyright © 2014 by **ANTHROTOURISM PRESS**. All rights reserved.
Editors: Jesse Casanova, Dr. Irvin Ziemann, & Ana Lucia Forero

2nd Edition designed and edited by Abigail Manheim.

Published in the United States of America

First print edition published 2014

Library of Congress Control Number: 2015909115

ISBN-13: 978-1512075380
ISBN-10: 1512075388

1. Business Economics/Foreign Exchange
2. Political Science/International Relations Trade & Tariffs

DEDICATION

This book is dedicated to two of the most influential and honorable individuals in my life: my grandparents. The advice and insight they imparted to me has encouraged me to live a life of passion and to pursue my dreams, no matter how unrealistic they may seem to others. Their words of encouragement and inspiration ultimately motivated me to take the risk and go to Cuba. Their wisdom and insight taught me that the power of my dreams and the desires of my heart are something that should never be suppressed, but rather made real. Their lives were an example of this passion for people and living. And it is an honor to dedicate this book to two people of such greatness.

CONTENTS

ACKNOWLEDGMENTS

The incentive for this publishing project was the result of a long-awaited research trip that I took to Cuba during the summer of 2012. The purpose of this trip was to learn about a culture that I had only read about in books and seen in documentaries and movies. To this end, I would like to express my deepest appreciation to the following individuals and groups:

First, my friend and the President of Southeastern University, Dr. Kent Ingle, for his recommendation letter in support of traveling to Cuba; the De La Rosa Travel Agency for making my trip seamless; my dear friend and colleague, Dr. Irvin Ziemann, for writing the prologue to this book; and my family and friends who supported me by believing in this trip. Next, I extend my deepest appreciation to my extremely kind and generous hosts, the various Cuban people with whom I stayed. Furthermore, my innermost gratitude extends to the United States' Customs and Travel Agency, U.S. and Cuban Governments and Cuban Customs for approval of this trip.

Alongside all of those mentioned above, special acknowledgement is given to all of the editors and designers at **Anthrotourism Press** for bringing this project to fruition.

Finally, I would like to say thank you to everyone that is not specifically mentioned here but is not forgotten. You all were the driving force that helped me do the impossible. This trip was life-changing; and I hope that the contents of this book will help others understand the beauty that is Cuba.

ABOUT THE AUTHOR

Jason Old is a full-time professor of Spanish and Latin American Culture at Southeastern University in Lakeland, Florida. He is also the CEO and co-founder of The SurfShare, LLC, a surf-sharing social networking platform whose mission is to connect surfers and surf enthusiasts from across the globe to foster more enjoyable surf travel, as well as to create economic sustainability in the coastal communities of the developing world. He has earned a Master's degree from the University of South Florida in Latin American, Caribbean, and Latino Studies, with concentrations in Anthropology and Spanish-American Literature.

When he is not teaching at the university, he travels around Latin America and enjoys the beauties of a region of the world that stole his heart almost 15 years ago. Jason has been fortunate enough to have lived in almost all of the Spanish-speaking countries of Latin America. When he is in Latin America, he is generally involved in one way or another with sport and development projects, field research, and extreme sports. Jason loves to travel and feed his never-ending desire to learn more about other cultures. He currently lives in Tampa, Florida.

PROLOGUE

WRITTEN BY DR. IRVIN ZIEMANN

More than half a century has gone by since Fidel Castro and his devoted followers seized control of Cuba. The world waited to see in which direction Castro would lead the country and the Americans became deeply disappointed as Castro almost immediately allied himself "in spirit" with the Soviet Union.

Under the dictatorial regime of Fulgencio Batista, the country had grown progressively more corrupt, but because Batista maintained "good relations" with the government of the United States, Cuba continued to receive military and financial support, in spite of widespread gambling, prostitution, and drug trafficking. At the same time, United States companies profited tremendously from their ownership of sugar lands, mines, cattle ranches, utilities, and oil.

Batista maintained a strong opposition to communism and thus remained in the good graces of the U. S. government. In the late 1950s, guerilla uprisings led to Batista's eventual defeat. Batista sought refuge in the Dominican Republic and eventually in Portugal. Under various titles, Fidel Castro then led the country from 1959 to 2008, nationalizing industry and business and declaring the country a socialist state. Although the United States had supported Batista because of his opposition to communism, his corruption had not been favored and government leaders were not disappointed to see his defeat. They envisioned a bright future for the young Fidel, but their enthusiasm turned to disappointment when Castro embraced the Soviet Union as his ally.

Thus began an uneasy relationship between the United States and Cuba, with signs of possible restoration of ties coming only in recent years. Because of the political separation of the two countries, Cuba has become an "unknown quantity" to the average American who reads or hears accounts which normally present only one side of Cuban life and politics. Because of this, we are fortunate to have such seekers after truth as Jason Old, a professor of Spanish at Southeastern University in Lakeland, Florida.

In 2012, Professor Old had two opportunities to spend extensive amounts of time in Cuba. The visits were not government sponsored; Old had the opportunity to view the country objectively—to experience life in all areas without being told what he must or must not see and how to interpret it.

This book is remarkably enlightening and objective. Professor Old not only gives us an unbiased look at government operations and financial and social affairs, but also shares with us the beauty and variety of the country. This book will give the reader a deeper understanding of the low and high points of life in Cuba, interspersed with descriptions of the natural beauty and the warmth of the people.

INTRODUCTION

Over the last ten years of my life, I have been intrigued with Cuba, its history, its people, its relationship with the United States, and most importantly, the Cuban Revolution itself. Perhaps it was the iconic Che face[1] that was on trendy Che Guevara T-shirts that I saw people wearing, even though many of them had no clue about the man behind the face on the front of their T-shirts. Maybe it was the ubiquity of those T-shirts that intrigued me enough to want to learn who he was, this man known worldwide as the inspirational guerilla fighter who stood up to imperialism. Or perhaps it was because I was obligated to read about him during my graduate school days in my Latin American, Caribbean, and Latino studies at the University of South Florida. No matter what the origin may have been, I have found myself captivated by the question of whether the man known as *el Che* was a good guy, a bad guy, or a little of both.

I wasn't the only person to wonder. When I showed some of my undergraduate language students a picture of the Ministry of Industry building in Havana, Cuba, which has a huge face of Che on the front, and asked them who this guy was, one of the students said, "That's Che." Then when I asked him, "What do you know about him?" he replied, "I am confused. Some tell me that he was a great guy, and others tell me that he was a murderer." Perhaps my student naively summarized Che's profound impact on Latin America and our ambivalence toward him. The truth is that it is a person's worldview, ideology, and perspective on humanity that determines, for that person, whether Che's impact on Latin America was positive or negative.

Che Guevara is a name that still stirs up controversy, as his ideology, which is primarily based on Marxist-Leninist[2] principles, is one that is seen as a threat to some, particularly the upper class, and a hope for others, notably the underprivileged. Whatever the origin of my interest, gaining an understanding of Che, of the precursors to the Cuban Revolution, and of the current sociopolitical system in post-revolution Cuba are the things that motivated me to travel to Cuba. I knew that in order to truly understand what has happened historically and what is happening now, I needed to go and see for myself.

Going to Cuba would allow me get a better perspective and understanding in order to help me answer some of my questions regarding one of the most provocative and iconic figures Latin America has seen over the last century—Ernesto Guevara de la Serna y Lynch, known by most people as Che[3] Guevara. His development and ideology as a human being have captivated me for years. And as a result of my interest in him as an iconic and intriguing Latin American figure, I have dedicated numerous years to studying his life, from his birth in 1928 in Rosario, Argentina, to his death in 1967 in the Bolivian countryside at the hands of the Bolivian National Army and the United States Central Intelligence Agency (CIA).

Studying the life of Che Guevara led me to study Cuba, its history and independence, its revolution, and its current political system. I studied them even more profoundly before making the trip to this intriguing island nation. Ultimately, the primary purpose of this book is to compare and contrast the difference between what I have read and watched in movies, books, and documentaries with actual life in post-revolution Cuba, in order to get an idea of what the revolution has created over the last fifty-three years.

The subsequent chapters will tell of eyewitness accounts, anec-dotes, and my experiences during my travels through Cuba. The information I gathered during this ethnographical research project came by way of personal interviews and my own experiences as I traveled across Cuba.

The trip was divided into two separate round trips of approximately one month each. The first part, which represents the first of the two trips, originates in Pinar del Río, the farthest western province of Cuba, and ends in Holguín. The second part of this adventure, which represents the second of the two trips, starts where I left off in Holguín, loops through *El Oriente,* the farthest eastern province of Cuba, and concludes once again in Holguín.

What makes this book unique is that I was born and raised in the United States, the imperialist power that has punished Cuba since John F. Kennedy[4] instituted a full-fledged economic trade embargo[5] on Cuba after the Cuban missile crisis in 1962. You might be tempted to excuse the United States for penalizing Cuba when they allowed the USSR to place nuclear weapons only ninety miles away from American soil. But before you nod your head in agreement, don't forget that the United States had nukes in Turkey aimed directly at the USSR.[6] After the crisis came to an uneasy close, Nikita Khrushchev[7] reached an agreement with Kennedy to remove the missiles on the condition that the United States agree never to invade Cuba. This agreement was reached without consulting the Cuban leaders, Fidel Castro and Che Guevara. This arbitrary decision[8] by the Soviets enraged the Cuban people, especially Fidel Castro and Che Guevara. Speaking about the nuclear weapons, Che allegedly said later that if it had been up to him, he would have launched them at the very heart of the United States, New York City.

My perspective is a bit different from many other Americans because I have taken the time to study this and subsequent events, and although I am not Cuban, or even Latino, I have been inspired by the revolution's ideology itself. Moreover, I have attempted to empathize with the revolutionaries and have sincerely tried to understand the purpose behind the Cuban Revolution itself in the most objective[9] way possible. Finally, studying Che Guevara's involvement in the Cuban Revolution and his subsequent roles in post-revolution Cuba as the head of the Ministry of Industry, the president of the Bank of Cuba, and the many other roles that he played before his departure from Cuba is particularly fascinating because he is not even from Cuba, but rather from Rosario,[10] Argentina, a city over three thousand miles away. What could his motivation have been?

Now that the restrictions[11] to travel to Cuba have loosened up a bit in the recent past, I thought that it would be a good idea to take a trip to Cuba to try to get a better perspective of how the Cuban people live within their own country, how they feel about their current socialist system, and what their opinions of Fidel and Raúl Castro are. I have also had the opportunity to talk to numerous Cuban-Americans in Tampa and Miami about their experiences in Cuba, their opinion of

Che Guevara and the Castros, and the revolution itself. These are Cubans who have sought political amnesty in the United States, and they have the freedom to speak their mind about their native Cuba. Many of them spoke poorly of the Cuban Revolution. Many of them empathized[12] with Batista, the dictator in power who was removed by Castro and his revolutionary forces in 1959. These were also often people who had benefitted from the Batista regime. However, I wanted to go see for myself. I knew that would be the only way to get an objective point of view of the revolution and its ideology.

In short, the purpose of this book is to shed a bit of light on the Cuban way of life. And even though this book does not speak for all Cubans, it will offer some insights into their society by highlighting both the good and the bad aspects of the Cuban system and way of life. Even after spending nearly ten years studying this island nation, I had no idea what to expect. No matter how much I had read and had academically understood about Cuba and its revolution, there was nothing that could have given me as clear a view of post-revolution Cuban life as going there in person to do this ethnographical research.

I invite you to join my *anthrotouristic*[13] journey through Cuba, as I seek to understand and describe Cuba's system, the culture, and the overall way of life. I am certain that this book will provide a better understanding of Cuba as you read about what it is like to live with Cuban families, talk with people in Cuba, and roam the streets of all its major cities.

For me, this was the opportunity of a lifetime, as most Americans did not have the luxury of flying directly from the United States to Cuba without risking huge fines and even jail time. So I am extremely thankful and indebted to both Cuba and the United States for allowing me the opportunity to go to such an amazing country to learn more about their way of life and their unique system of government. It is my hope that this book will provide you with a deeper insight and understanding into the Cuban society, their people, their government, and their culture.

WELCOME
TO CUBA

When I first got the itinerary for my trip to Cuba, I thought that the day was going to start out extremely early because I saw 9:15 a.m. on my plane ticket; however, I found that was just the time I needed to arrive at the airport to check my luggage in at the counter. It turned out that my plane wasn't leaving until 1:15 p.m. I was a bit curious as to why the travel agency wanted me to arrive at 9:15 a.m., hours ahead of my flight time, even assuming that it would leave on time! Nevertheless, I eagerly got there by 9:30 a.m. and quickly found out why it was advisable to arrive that early. It was because everyone who travels to Cuba takes suitcases full of clothes, medicines, TVs, and anything else they could find at Wal-Mart or Target to "import" into Cuba for their family members who are still living in there, without access to the many products Americans take for granted.

I would venture to say that almost everyone there, except me, had at least three to five duffel bags full of additional goods to check in—sometimes even more. Although I was surprised by the scenario at first, given what I understood about Cuba, it made sense. No average citizen in Cuba could afford a brand-new forty-inch flat-screen TV, even if it could be found in the stores. The average Cuban—even a doctor—earns less than $70 USD a month. So buying a luxury item such as a forty-inch flat-screen TV is out of the question for most people living there. But since that was none of my business, and since I had bigger things to worry about, I left my headphones on and hoped that once I got to the counter, they wouldn't give me any trouble for being an American trying to travel to Cuba. With all that luggage, the line moved incredibly slowly, but when I eventually made it to the counter an hour and a half later, I was greeted only with a smiling face and a lack of any problems. I thought to myself, *That seemed all too easy.*

Rather than question my good fortune, I grabbed my carry-on bag without further ado and made my way upstairs to Security. I was now assuming that I would run into problems with the TSA (Transportation Safety Administration) or someone who took issue with the fact that I was going to Cuba directly from the USA,[14] which in this day and age, despite the history between the United States and Cuba and the trade embargo, seemed surreal. Many people assume it is not possible for Americans to travel to Cuba at all, but what most people do not realize is that there are legitimate ways to go to Cuba legally. These ways are just not necessarily available for all Americans. There are certain "general" and "special" visas provided to Americans who wish to travel to Cuba. Fortunately for me, one of those general visas allowed me to travel to Cuba for academic purposes in order to do research about Cuba's remarkable history. As it turned out, having all of the proper documentation made my interaction with Cuban customs largely seamless.

After clearing security with no challenges whatsoever, and after boarding the plane, finding my seat, and settling into it, it finally sank in that I was going to Cuba for real. I sat back in my seat (alone in the emergency row) and enjoyed my one-hour flight from Tampa, Florida, to Havana, Cuba. I was the only American-born person on the plane. It was full of men, women, and children who were all excited to return to Cuba. Many of them had not returned in over 15 years. As we were approaching Havana, I began to get a bit nervous again because I could not be sure that I was going to be let into the country. Although I had filled out all of the correct paperwork, and everyone had assured me I would be fine, there was no real guarantee that when I landed I would be allowed in. I would have to get there and find out. Nevertheless, there was nothing I could do now, so I did my best just to sit back and enjoy the view and the smooth landing. To my surprise, as we landed, everyone on the plane began to clap, ecstatic to be returning to the country they had left for one reason or another. I found myself a bit overwhelmed with emotion as well, with the display of heartfelt joy from these Cuban-Americans, my fellow passengers.

Then the real moment of truth came as we disembarked from the plane and made our way toward Customs and Immigration. I was grinning from cheek to cheek, knowing that if all went well, I was about to enter Cuba and do something that very few Americans will ever get to do: simply to visit this country and see firsthand how the much-vilified Cuban system actually works, and get the actual opinions of real citizens who live in Castro's Cuba. As I got closer to the Customs area and prepared to give the official my passport, I grew nervous again, wondering what questions the officer might ask me and what reaction she would have when she saw that I was an American citizen.

Yet, to my surprise, my interaction with the Customs officer was short and sweet, and in no way difficult. As I said *"Gracias,"* I walked through the door, passed my carry-on luggage through the x-ray machine, and showed the next officer my passport. *"Americano?"*[15] he asked me, and I quickly responded, *"Sí."* He then said, "Thanks and welcome to Cuba," in Spanish, of course.

And now, finally, I was about to officially set foot in Cuba and be on my way to my *casa particular*[16]—that's a government-approved "home stay," which serves as an alternative to staying in a hotel. The concept of the *casa particular* in Cuba is an idea that has come about in the recent past as a result of the influx of tourism into the country. Interestingly, the *casa particular* concept is a private endeavor, or business, run and operated by an individual or family. Of course the owner of the *casa particular* pays a relatively heavy tax on their *casa*, but it is still a privately-owned business that essentially competes with the State for the tourist trade. The other option for visitors is to stay in a State-run hotel.

Note that, interestingly, the use of the word *particular* in Cuba to refer to private, or capitalist, enterprise (e.g., *casa particular, restaurante particular, taxi particular,* etc.) is similar to the use of the word *public* by Americans to refer to state-subsidized, or socialized, endeavors. The assumption in the U.S. is that a business is private unless otherwise specified; in Cuba, the assumption is exactly the opposite. A business is public unless it is specifically stated to be *particular*.

Before I could start my adventure, I had to grab my checked luggage, which seemed as though it was never going to come out onto the conveyor belt. Eventually, though in its own good time, it appeared, and I was able to go through the last security checkpoint, exchange my money, and find Julio, my taxi driver, who was waiting for me just outside the door.

I greeted Julio with a great sigh of relief, barely able to believe that I was officially standing on Cuban soil. It was incredible! Interestingly enough, and within less than five minutes of being in Cuba, I was greeted by one of the most provocative billboards I had ever seen. And even though it could be seen as anti-American in nature, I just looked at it objectively and smiled serenely as we drove out of the airport parking lot and headed to the hotel. It was a gigantic black billboard with large letters saying, *"El Bloqueo"* ("The Embargo"). A picture of the island of Cuba sat in the middle of the black background. A noose dangled from the top of the billboard, and the country of Cuba sat in the middle of the noose. It was a very interesting and eloquent message, and it gave me an opening to talk to Julio about Cuba's political system, his perspective on his country, and what he thought about the United States as well. As it turned out, he had no more perspective on the "real" U.S. than most Americans have on the "real" Cuba.

While we drove to my *casa particular* in Vedado, which is a part of Central Havana, we talked about Cuba, its health care and education systems, and their two major sports, soccer and baseball. Baseball is still undoubtedly the country's most popular sport, but I couldn't help noticing that all of the kids in the parks we passed were playing soccer, not baseball, as we drove approximately twenty minutes from the airport into the center of Havana. It was an eye-opening conversation, as I soaked in all that Julio was telling me.

He told me that if he were to need open-heart surgery, it would be free. He would just have to get the proper approval and set up an appointment just like you would in most, if not all, places around the world. Of course a doctor needs to have done proper testing and to have determined what type of surgery is needed, and this assessment would also be done for free. That to me was mind-blowing, as it would be to any American, considering that a procedure like that in the U.S. is expensive even for people who have health insurance, and would be virtually impossible for people without insurance to afford. The cost for the surgery alone in the U.S. would be between $100,000 and $120,000 or more, depending on the procedure and the length of the surgery, and that might not include the hospitalization and doctor fees, and other adjunct care that would be needed.

After arriving at the *Casa de Juliet* in Central Havana, I went upstairs and met my host. This house was less like a home stay and more like a hostel than I had imagined. This *casa particular* was set up this way intentionally, which is the reason I chose to stay there upon my arrival in Havana. That way, I would be able to meet other fellow travelers and they could point me in the right direction in terms of getting to know the city, its places, and its people.

However, even more important than all of that was the UEFA (Union of European Football Associations) Champions League finals, which was on TV when I got to *Casa de Juliet*. I had missed most of regular time because I was flying when the game officially started. In any case, I made it to Havana and to my *casa* just in time to see overtime and the grand finale, which was better than nothing—not to mention that it was an amazing ending: Chelsea FC (England) beat Bayern Munich (Germany) in a penalty shoot-out.

After the game, I wanted to get out and explore Havana, so my new friends, Bhumi, TC, Kine, Sandra, and I walked down to *El Hotel Nacional* (the National Hotel), which is not only a beautiful hotel in the neighborhood of Vedado, but is also a historical landmark and a must-see for anyone who comes to Havana. Bhumi and TC are close friends from London who came to Cuba to travel a bit and hang out in Havana and the surrounding cities. Kine and Sandra are sisters from Norway, and after Kine had been traveling through South America for about seven months, she met up with her sister in Central America. After exploring Central America a bit, they came to Cuba. It was a pleasure to get to meet them and hang out with them. They took me down to *El Hotel Nacional* and the *Malecón* to show me around, and also so I could send an e-mail home, using the services of an Internet café, to let everyone know that I arrived and all was well. The *Malecón* is a bulkhead that runs the length of Havana's coastline, taking you from one end of the city to the other. It has a huge wall and a nice sidewalk where locals and tourists like us hang out, talk, sing, and dance into all hours of the night. The *Malecón* is also accompanied by a road that is heavily trafficked by Cubans who travel around Havana. It is like a mini-Pacific Coast Highway, except that it is only about ten miles long.

Despite its size, it is certainly a great place to spend time in order to get the true flavor of local Havana culture.

One night after walking around the *Malecón* and hanging out at the hotel, I managed to convince Kine and Sandra to sit at the *casa* after dinner and watch a documentary about Che Guevara with me. We had a great time drinking Cuban coffee together and watching a documentary about Che in Cuba. The documentary was on a DVD that the owner of the *casa*, Andy, owned. It was one of only three DVDs in his possession. Clearly, our options were limited. In fact, the other two DVDs were about Cuba too. We decided to watch a DVD only after perusing the five[17] channels that make up Cuban TV. After failing to find anything else of interest to watch, we decided that a DVD about Che Guevara was the best option we had.

It turned out that Andy, Juliet's husband, actually used to work at *El Hotel Nacional*. He worked there for approximately ten years where he dealt with tourists. As a result, he had a wealth of knowledge about Havana, as well as a great perspective on the Cuban economic and political system. After he made dinner for all of us—I ate a huge lobster dish for $8—we talked a bit about politics, and I came to find out that, contrary to American perception, there is a certain level of freedom that Cubans have in talking about the revolution and the system that is currently in place here in Cuba. So I was relieved to find that we could speak freely and not worry about being hauled off to jail or deported, which was, I admit, a preconceived notion that I had about Cuba. Although it was true that in certain cases one might get hauled off to jail for speaking freely, it was not the norm, according to Andy.

From Juliet, who was also there talking to us, I found out that before she opened this *casa particular*, she was a professor at the University of Havana for sixteen years, where she taught sociology and linguistics classes. Since that is more or less the same subjects that I teach back in the United States, I had the enlightening experience of being able to compare the different teaching curricula, pedagogies, and even salaries with her.

For example, I learned that a professor in Cuba earns less than $30 a month. Of course, his or her education, health care, and housing are essentially free. Also, like all Cubans, they are given a certain monthly ration of food (*La Canasta Básica*[18]), free of charge from the government, *(el Estado,* or "the State"). This is a right guaranteed not only to all State workers, but to all Cuban citizens. Despite these benefits, she decided that she would like to start a *casa particular* and entertain tourists because it is more profitable and allows her and her husband to better provide for their family (Andy also has another day job). And they were good at it, too—they did a wonderful job of making me feel immediately welcomed and part of the family.

GETTING TO KNOW HAVANA

One evening, while I was in Havana, I had the chance to have a conversation with our hostel owners about who the "millionaires" are in Cuba. According to them, it is the private, or *particular*, taxi drivers. The reason for this is that, even though the taxi drivers have to pay taxes just like everyone else, the tax-to-income ratio for a taxi driver allows the taxi drivers to profit much more than most Cuban professionals, such as nurses, professors, and doctors. A private taxi pays approximately $50 a month in taxes. Yet, a taxi driver who works eight hours a day, six days a week, can do very well, relative to the $15 a month a physical therapist makes, or even the $50 a month a doctor earns. In fact, it could be said that a successful taxi driver makes more than a professional[19] athlete makes in Cuba.

Here is how it works: private (non-State) taxi drivers operate as a capitalist business, in that they have the freedom to earn as much money as they can. In other words, if they work hard, they will do well, financially speaking. However, at the end of the month, the taxi driver is responsible for paying a flat tax to the government for his or her private business "permit." This approach is essentially the same as it is in most countries where business owners pay a business tax to the government. Interestingly, this flat tax can be advantageous to non-State taxi drivers who work hard and make well above the flat tax set forth by the State. That tax is generally around $50; still, anything that is earned above and beyond that tax is net income for the taxi driver.

The private taxi drivers who drive tourists from the airport to Havana and around other parts of Cuba do very well. For example, a twenty-minute ride from the airport to Central Havana costs $20. A taxi driver who makes two and a half round trips to the airport has covered his or her government tax for the month. Now anything that he or she makes above that can be kept.

A doctor, for example, is paid approximately fifty CUC and has to work all day, every day. (The value of the Cuban convertible peso [CUC] to United States dollar [USD] is one to one; I will be discussing how this exchange rate is not quite accurate in a later chapter.) Now let's not forget that a doctor does not have to pay for his or her studies—education would be covered all the way through medical school—his or her apartment, or any of the other day-to-day needs. This is theoretically speaking, of course, as there are still needs that come along with studying. However, typically the responsibility to meet those needs is shouldered by the parents of the student. This increases the burden on the parents, who, by and large, are struggling to get by in the first place. That is, of course, unless they are getting outside help, or remittances, sent to them from a relative living in the United States or another country.

Owning a house or paying rent is of concern to most people in both the developing world as well as the developed world. Everybody needs a home. So I was curious to know how Andy and Juliet were able to afford their *casa particular,* which was actually two adjacent apartments that they converted into one giant establishment. The way it worked in their individual case was the following: Their three-bedroom, two-bathroom *casa* cost them a grand total of approximately $200 for the house (over the course of the rest of your life—see it as a mortgage like we have in the USA). Yet, you can pay whatever sum of money you want every month. Furthermore, if you do not even have one dollar to pay in a particular month, it is okay just to pay it the following month. This may not be the case for everyone, as many people build a house by stages, which is the only way to avoid owing money on one's house. In fact, as I came to find out as I traveled across the country, it seemed that building a house in stages was by far the more popular route people chose. A third option was to get the house "passed down" through an inheritance. Nevertheless, with regard to Juliet's *casa* in particular, she told me that if she does not pay her business tax of approximately $200 per month to the State for her *casa particular*, she gets a fine. This tax must be paid whether or not she has guests. Taxes are levied by the room, not by the amount of money she earned that particular month. If she fails to pay the monthly tax for her private business, she will receive a knock on the door by the tax police issuing her a fine, or penalty, for failure to pay her tax on time. Eventually, if she were to fail to pay over the course of a handful of months, she would run the risk of losing her business. To put it into capitalist terms, it would be similar to going into bankruptcy or foreclosure. From what I gathered, the taxes that are paid to the State are then allocated to public services such as schools, clinics, hospitals, and even road maintenance.

Another topic that I had the chance to discuss with Andy and Juliet was the concept of *freedom of speech*, which is something that many Americans do not think exists in Cuba (this will be a theme that is discussed in more depth throughout the rest of the book). According to my hosts, and contrary to popular American belief, you can actually express yourself *freely* with regard to politics. However, most Cubans know what they can and cannot get away with saying with regard to their opinion towards the government. The Cuban people have created hand gestures when they want to talk about their "Maximum Leader," Fidel Castro. For instance, when they stroke their chin while talking, as if they had a beard, this represents Fidel.

So the idea that they have the *freedom* to express themselves regarding their opinion of the current administration is debatable. Still, the fact that they can, to a certain degree, express themselves at all, is more than I expected. But don't forget that not everyone is against the Castro administration. There are a large number of supporters who have benefited tremendously from the revolution. One of those people is Andy's father, who, before the revolution, had no access to a real education, doctors, or anything else that the current administration brought into fruition after the triumph of the revolution in 1959.

I had the opportunity to sit and spend a number of hours talking with Andy's father. Before the revolution, they lived out in the impoverished Cuban countryside, lacking access to doctors and nurses, quality teachers, and with little options to make a living and buy food.

As a result of the revolution and its socialist ideology, they were given access to a decent education, food, and housing. And because of that, they were extremely supportive of Castro and the revolution itself. It was a privilege to have the opportunity to talk to him about the way things were pre-revolution versus how things are now. Of course, as we both agreed, there is no country in the world that is perfect, though each country has wonderful things to offer as well as challenges its citizens must cope with. The problem for Cuba is that, as a result of its adversarial history with the United States and its uniqueness in terms of its political and economic ideology, it has become an easy target for criticism, mainly because countries like the United States, and the individuals who lobby to keep the embargo as is, want to see Cuba fail, rather than admit that a socialist country can work. Whether or not the system is truly a failure will be explored throughout the book, as I attempt to understand the intricacies of Cuba, its people, its culture, and its system.

One of the achievements that Cuba inarguably has the right to brag about would be their extremely low illiteracy rate, which ranges between 1 percent and .5 percent. That means that almost 100 percent of the population is able to read and write at a basic level. They are actually ranked as a country with one of the highest literacy rates in the world. That is better than the United States, whose literacy rate usually ranges around 98 percent, which is still not bad, considering that the United States has a population of approximately 300 million. What makes Cuba's literacy rate such an unexpected statistic is that it is an underdeveloped country, whereas the United States and other countries with high literacy rates are developed. A high literacy rate is to be expected in those countries. After all, the developed countries theoretically have the money to invest in education. Another interesting accolade for Cuba is that one of their main exports is not a natural resource, but rather people. Cuba is famous for sending doctors, nurses, teachers, and even troops to other parts of the developing world. For example, Cuba has, in the recent past, sent a large quantity of Cuban doctors to Haiti to help train Haitians, as well as to perform medical procedures in order to offset the fact that Haiti is unable to provide sufficient medical services for their citizens.

An interesting thing happened to us as we walked out into the street from our hostel. I was with some British friends whom I had met in the hostel, and one of them had a bag full of pencils and pens that he wanted to give to a school so that the students could have some extra supplies. My British friend asked me to ask the school across the street from our hostel if they needed pens or pencils for their students. Of course they said yes, and were excited to take this generous gift. As a thank-you, they invited us into the school so that they could show us their classes and classrooms, what they do, and what type of students they work with. It turned out to be a school for students with learning disabilities. I told them that my mom works with special education students back in the United States. There was a bit of joking about the fact that I was an American in Cuba, but it was all in good humor, and I laughed along with everyone else.

I called their attention to the José Martí statue that adorned the entrance of the courtyard, and they began talking to me about their country's heroes. Then I told them that I live in Tampa, Florida, and that Tampa was a place where José Martí spent time and even gave a very famous speech in Ybor City. The place where Martí gave that speech—*El Parque de los Amigos*—still stands as a testament to the impact that Martí had, in Florida as well as in Cuba. Unfortunately, shortly after this monumental speech in Tampa, José Martí was killed on May 19, 1895 by the Spanish, in the first battle for Cuba's independence.

They were curious to know how and why I knew so much about José Martí, Fidel and Raúl Castro, and Che Guevara. They were surprised that I knew so much about Cuban history and the revolution as well. The next thing I knew, I found myself in the office of the director, as she was trying to load me up with books about the revolution, while talking nonstop about her country, her government, and her school. It ended with her settling for giving me only one book and extracting a promise that I would come back tomorrow to see the students. Before we left, the director showed us the projects that her students made with different materials they had available: old cans, plastic, etc. One of the students had made an artificial flower arrangement, which was hanging on the wall. After the show-and-tell, I made a comment about the Che and Fidel posters in the school office, and we started talking about the revolution and Cuba's history. They all lit up, eager to talk about their country's leader, Fidel Castro (though Raúl Castro took over in 2008 because of Fidel's deteriorating health). I took home the book, which was about the revolution, read it thoroughly, and then returned it to them two days later. Even though schools are accessible for all and boast an extremely high literacy rate, Cuba is still a developing country, and access to resources is limited.

Before our encounter with the people at the school, we had planned to set out on a trip to one of the Spanish forts that stands at the end of the *Malecón* in Havana. Actually, it was across the Bay of Havana (*La Bahía de Havana*), so we had to go through a tunnel to get to the other side in order to visit the fort, which was called *Castillo de los Tres Reyes del Morro*. It was a beautiful fort that was built and had its glory days from about 1589 to 1640, which was when the Spanish had begun to fortify Cuba against the British—or anyone else who dared to get near. In most cases, the Spanish, and particularly Columbus, who sailed for the Spanish (he was actually Italian by birth), typically renamed the places that they "discovered" in order to give honor and glory to God and to the Spanish crown (e.g., Borinquen was changed to Puerto Rico). In the case of Cuba, for one reason or another, they chose to leave it with its indigenous Taino name, Cuba.

After checking out the *Castillo* and walking around the grounds, we made our way, via a 1950s Chevrolet taxi, to the *Museo de la Revolución* (the Museum of the Revolution) and *Havana Vieja* (Old Town Havana). Interestingly enough, these 1950s automobiles, here in Cuba, cost approximately $10,000–$20,000, depending on the make and model of the car. These cars remained in Cuba after the revolution, and from that point forward, the United States–as a result of the embargo–has never shipped another car to Cuba. Since they have no access to original parts, they have to be creative in how they preserve these beautiful cars. In fact, some of them do not even have the original engines (as you might imagine), and so they have replaced them with Hyundai engines or another engine that came from Asia. I was amazed at how these taxi drivers were able to maintain these cars in such spectacular condition. Riding in these cars was like stepping back in time. It was, without a doubt, an exciting way to travel around Havana.

After enjoying our ride in the 1950s Chevrolet, we were dropped off near *El Prado* in front of the Museum of the Revolution and relatively close to *Havana Vieja*—certainly within walking distance. For me, the museum was a special attraction, as one of my purposes in coming to Cuba was to learn about the Cuban Revolution firsthand. The museum was full of information about the revolution, pictures and weapons from the revolution, and even a wax figure set of Camilo Cienfuegos and Che Guevara in action. It was like looking at two giant action figures. And of course the museum was adorned with José Martí statues that remind the visitor of the original revolutionary, *el Apostle* (the Apostle), José Martí. Martí was one of the intellectuals responsible for bringing about Cuba's War of Independence against Spain, though he was killed in 1895, approximately three years before Cuba's victory.

From the museum, we walked around the back of the building to see the *Granma*, the boat that was taken by Fidel and Che's men from the coast of Mexico to Cuba, preserved in commemoration of the arrival of the eighty-two men who came to reclaim Cuba from Batista in the late 1950s. Unfortunately for them, of the eighty-two men who arrived, shipwrecked, at Las Coloradas with only a handful of guns between them, only twelve survived the waiting ambush by Batista's men. The twelve remaining survivors, among them Fidel and Raúl Castro, Camilo Cienfuegos, and Che Guevara, eventually regrouped and managed to overthrow Batista and his men, sending Batista fleeing to the Dominican Republic and into the arms of his friend, Rafael Trujillo.[20] And whether or not you strongly support or staunchly oppose this historical event, the Cuban Revolution, in overthrowing the U.S.-backed Batista government, was an amazing feat that was accomplished against all odds by Fidel and his men. I could not get over thinking about what these men achieved. And as I continued to travel across the country and as I learned more and more, I was constantly blown away by the passion that they must have had to create a better Cuba for everyone.

In keeping with the theme of exploring Havana, we went to *Havana Vieja*, which was pretty full of tourists navigating through the narrow colonial streets and exploring the older part of Cuba. This was where Ernest Hemingway spent much of his time when he lived in Cuba. Hemingway was a supporter of the revolution and was friends with

Fidel Castro. Unfortunately, this great American writer took his own life as a result of depression. Some speculate that, although he had been married multiple times, he was not entirely over his first love, which, as a result of mixing alcohol with depression, led him to end his life by shooting himself in the chest. Be that as it may, he is well known in Cuba, particularly in Old Havana. He frequented the bar known as *La Floridita*, which is still open for business today, and where Hemingway is known for holding the record for consuming the most daiquiris in one sitting. They have since then named a drink after him, "The Papa Double." "Papa," or "Papa Hemingway," was Hemingway's nickname. He also lived at *Ambos Mundos*, a hotel in the heart of *Havana Vieja*. This hotel stands out among the other buildings, as it is pink and extremely beautiful. After visiting it and having a *café americano* there, I realized that they had some of the best *café americanos* in all of Havana, and believe me, I became an expert. I am not sure if Hemingway drank the *café americanos* or just the simple, yet famous, *café cubano* (espresso and sugar). But nevertheless, he certainly had good taste in choosing this place to live.

Aside from these tributes to Hemingway, *Havana Vieja* also offers people great places to eat, hang out, and even buy books about Cuba, its history, and its historical figures. The books were set out by individual vendors who lined the cobblestone streets in a small section of *Havana Vieja* and sold these books inexpensively to Cubans and tourists alike. After looking at the books, Bhumi, TC, and I decided to get something to eat. And after being escorted into a rather nice restaurant—which was outside of my backpacker's budget—we had a great meal.

Great meal aside, we were lucky (or unlucky) enough to see something that was a bit disturbing. While we were eating our chicken, a peacock came up to the table and stole Bhumi's chicken and began to eat it. I think that makes the peacock a cannibal, no? We were taken aback because to think that a bird is eating another bird was just weird. And after entertaining ourselves by watching the peacock eat chicken, we asked for *la cuenta* (the check) and called it a day by heading back to the *casa*.

JULIET AND HER SON

One of the dilemmas that have come about as a result of *el bloqueo* is the divided family. What is interesting about this is that, in many cases, one could even have a father or a mother living in Cuba, and the other parent living in the USA. Sometimes the family member living in the USA is granted asylum, residency, and ultimately, citizenship, and then they come back to visit their family members in Cuba or send them *remesas* (or remittances). These individuals generally bring back gifts and necessities for their relatives in Cuba, as getting luxury items here on their own accord is out of the question—hence all of the people checking in giant duffel bags at the airport. This is pretty standard behavior for people who live in these two worlds. I have a friend whose parents actually went through the trouble of getting divorced just so that they could each marry U.S. citizens in order to bring their family to the U.S. One could only imagine what type of confusion this would cause children who have to act like their mother's new husband is their real father. Still, these are some of the measures that many Cubans are willing to take in order to move their family out of Cuba. I am not saying that I condone this type of behavior; rather, I wish to show the lengths that many Cubans are willing to take in order to leave their own country for one reason or another.

On the other hand, there is another group of people who are living in the States who have pretty much cut ties from Cuba altogether, and are trying to convince other family members to follow suit in order to pursue a life of luxury. Unfortunately, achieving "the American Dream" is not as easy as many of these Cubans make it sound to their family members living back in Cuba. In fact, in most cases, it is unachievable. There are some places, such as Miami, Tampa, and New York, among other cities, that lend themselves to new immigrants who do not speak English. However, many people who leave the island as highly qualified professionals in Cuba find themselves working hard labor jobs or having to take positions such as custodian once they get to the United States. This is not because they are not qualified to work in their field in the USA; but rather because they do not speak English, and therefore cannot work in the career for which they were trained in Cuba. In addition, their Cuban degree is generally not valued here in the United States.

Juliet's son is being sold on the American dream by his biological father, who lives in Miami, Florida. He sends pictures of himself standing in downtown Miami with all the skyscrapers in the background, hanging out in South Beach, walking along luxurious yacht harbors, and so on. In other words, he is selling him a dream that is only realized by a small number, and unfortunately for the father, he doesn't belong to that small number either. Nevertheless, he continues to present this image, or façade, of luxury and materialism as a way to persuade the youngster to run away to the USA. Even though he has sent pictures and fed him this "life of luxury" rhetoric, according to his son and Juliet, he doesn't even have a credit card or enough money to call his own son. Interesting, right? On the other hand, Juliet is working day and night to provide for her son who lives in Cuba with her and her new husband, Andy, who not only has a full-time job himself, but also comes home after work to help run the *casa particular*. In the meantime, Juliet's son is in the top three of his class at his school. This means he is in the top three out of over one thousand students. As a result of his academic performance, he has been offered a full scholarship to attend one of the best schools in Cuba, which is run by the government and is responsible for "equipping the next generation of Cuban leaders." Of course Juliet wants him to stay in Cuba, because studying at this school, which will open doors for his future, is a wonderful career path in the eyes of his mother. If you remember, Juliet was a language and literature professor for sixteen years at the University of Havana. Now she owns her own business, the *casa* where I stayed. So of course she understands the importance of education and naturally wants the best for her son.

Here is the catch: if Juliet's son goes to the USA on a sojourn visa, for example, he would lose his offer to study at this elite government university. And in turn, he would presumably lose out on an opportunity to have a bright future in Cuba. And if he goes to Miami in search of a better life, then he may have a great deal of difficulty because he does not speak English. In all reality, not speaking English is no problem in Miami, as one would be able to get by in the day-to-day; however, if an individual would like to go beyond the Spanish-speaking community of Miami and branch out in search of a career outside of Dade County, then English is not only strongly recommended, but mandatory.

The thought of moving to Miami is extremely tempting, but, what Juliet's son is being shown by her ex-husband is not the Miami that he would live in, should he decide to abandon Cuba and move to the USA. This is a problem many Cubans are facing because of the embargo and the unfriendly bilateral relations between the USA and Cuba since the early 1960s. The interesting part about the embargo is that a large percentage of the Cuban exiles—the ones who left directly after the revolution to avoid being thrown in jail—are the ones who have consistently been lobbying to keep the U.S. trade embargo against Cuba in place, even though many of their relatives and family still live in Cuba.

I understand the resentment that they have toward the Castro administration. After all, as a result of the revolution, most of them lost a fortune when over 500 million dollars in assets were nationalized. These people were largely partnered with or working for U.S. companies in Cuba and living a very comfortable life. The problem is that only a small minority were living this way, and the Cuban Revolution was inspired by the idea of creating a more equal society (that is, a Marxist society) with the grand ideal of creating the *new man*, an idea promoted by Che Guevara after the revolution. Whether or not one agrees with that particular ideology is one's own personal opinion. However, one must analyze the success of the system, taking into account a number of factors: (1) Are more people benefiting from the ideology than before the revolution? (2) Does the ideology work well in Cuba? (3) Are the majority of the people happy with the system? (4) Is it meeting people's basic needs and allowing them the opportunity to succeed within their society? (5) Does it guarantee equal rights (e.g., education, health care, etc.) to all?

This is not an easy answer to get, because there are varying answers even among the Cuban people themselves. You will see this become clearer in subsequent chapters. The biggest mistake that one can make is to compare Cuba to the United States. Cuba is a developing country with little to no natural resources and very little economic influence on an international level. On the other hand, the United States is an extremely developed nation with an internationally respected currency—the United States dollar—and negotiating power on an international scale. According to the World Bank, Cuba's GDP (Gross Domestic Product) was approximately 68 billion dollars in 2011, whereas the United States' GDP was 15.5 trillion dollars. Therefore, it is not reasonable to compare one with the other. Rather, a better way to compare Cuba (or the United States) is by comparing these countries with their colleague countries. For example, given that Cuba is a developing country, it would be better to compare the general quality of life of the Cuban people to a country such as Nicaragua, Angola, Haiti, or Guatemala, in order to see how Cuba compares to other countries in its class. At the same time, if one wants to compare the United States to another country, then compare it to an economically developed country such as Germany, England, or France. That is the only way to correctly assess these countries. It is unfair to compare Cuba with the United States because you are comparing, first and foremost, a developing country such as Cuba with a developed country—in this case, the United States. Perhaps you could theoretically compare the overall quality of life in each country, although that may lead to a surprising answer. I mean, ask yourself, would you consider average Americans living in the United States to be happy with what they have? Similarly, you could ask that same question of the average Cuban. From there, one could theoretically ascertain whether or not the system in place allows their citizens to live a happy and meaningful life. And judging from the interviews I have had with people—and I interviewed a wide range of Cubans—I got a wide variety of answers with regard to quality of life, contentment, opinion of education, health care, and "freedom" (this is in quotation marks because *freedom* is a relative term which depends very much on how you define it). Furthermore, if we are going to assess Cuba and its system against the rest of the developing world, most of which has been subject to U.S. involvement since the Monroe Doctrine (1823) and Platt Amendment (1901), one could say that the gap between rich and poor has increased consistently in these countries over this time period. While that is not the point of this chapter, it is still good food for thought.

It might be suggested that if one were to objectively compare Cuba's quality of life for all Cubans versus the quality of life for all Nicaraguans, Angolans, or Haitians, for example, the statistics would probably show that Cubans, on average, are better off than the citizens of the previously mentioned countries, taking into consideration the average citizen's access to health care, education, housing, and food. Given my observations and conversations with the Cuban people, in addition to my fieldwork in other Latin American countries (I have done fieldwork in every Spanish-speaking country in Latin America except Paraguay), one could arguably make the assertion that the average Cuban has a better quality of life than the average citizen of most of the other countries in Latin America, particularly Central America. I know that is a very ambitious thing to say; however, if you are of the lower class of any other Latin American nation, it is hard to get quality health care, go to a quality school and get a quality education, afford a quality house made of concrete, and have consistent access to food. This is not to say that all Cubans live better than all other Latin Americans, because that would be an incorrect assertion. Naturally, a person of the upper class in Latin America is living well, and presumably has all of the amenities that any upper-class person would have, even in most parts of the developed world. Yet, a person of the lower class in Latin America has little to no upward mobility, and therefore the system only serves to perpetuate this cycle of poverty that has imprisoned the people of the developing world who are not aligned with the right multinational or national corporations.

IN AND AROUND HAVANA

We went to Tropicoco Beach near Tarará with TC, Bhumi, Sandra, and Kine for the day. This is the community where Che Guevara took up residence after the revolution; he said he needed to be near the ocean because the saltwater breeze was good for his asthma. Tropicoco is one of a number of beaches called *"La Playa del Este,"* which at approximately forty minutes outside of Havana, are the closest beaches to the city. They are very beautiful beaches, and when we went, they were not very crowded. Apparently, we were there during the off season. In any case, it was the closest beach that we could find, and it was pleasantly inexpensive to have the taxi drive us there in his souped-up 1950s Chevrolet. He had made some minor alterations to the car, so it wasn't absolutely authentic, as the car was equipped with AC and a nice stereo system.

We decided to test it out. At Kine's request, we hunted down her new favorite song, a Brazilian song from Michel Telo she incorrectly called *"Nossa."* When I asked the taxi driver to play the song, I asked for it by the official title, *"Si Eu Te Pego."* Surprisingly, the driver had no clue what I was talking about. However, when I told him that some people (particularly Kine) called it *"Nossa,"* he knew exactly what we were looking for. And once he found it on his burnt DVD mixed tape (yes, he had a DVD player in the car), he played it incessantly all the way there. He liked it so much that after he dropped us off, I was sure that he was going to play it repeatedly on the way home so he could sing it at the top of his lungs. On the way there, I translated the song for him from Portuguese to Spanish—not that I speak Portuguese well at all; I was able to understand what the singer was saying because he simply says the same thing over and over again throughout the whole song.

After returning from the beach, we got back to our *casa* in Havana, and I quickly got cleaned up to go to the house of a cousin of a friend mine from Tampa. They lived in Jaimanitas, near Miramar, outside of the center of Havana. I planned to have dinner with them and to deliver some gifts from their cousin back in Florida that I had brought them from the United States.

Dinner with Juan and his family was delicious. On the menu was *pargo* (snapper), vegetables, rice, beans, and potatoes. It was one of the first times that I had actually been on my own while eating in a proper Cuban household. Of course, I would consider all of my interactions at Juliet's *casa* authentic; however, this was one of the first times that I was alone with a Cuban family and was able to eat at their house. It was an unforgettable experience that allowed me to get a bit more insight into the heart of a working-class Cuban family. Since the other reason for meeting with them was to give them some gifts from the United States that Juan's cousin asked me to bring, it was a mutually beneficial meeting, which led to a great dinner and a very open and sincere conversation about Cuba, its people, its history, and its current government. Also, Juan showed me pictures taken when he used to work on the boat of a rich Italian, and they spent time hunting lobsters in Cayo Largo (Key Largo), which is off the southern coast of Cuba (not to be confused with Key Largo in Florida, USA). I later found out that it is illegal for the locals to hunt, capture, and eat the lobsters here without a fishing permit, because lobster-catching is only for the tourists, according to the individual that I interviewed.

The dinner and conversation with Juan and his family was unique, and ended with him removing a key from a key chain and giving me the chain. This was not *any* ordinary key chain; rather, it was an old picture of Che purifying river water with a can and a fire. Earlier that evening, I had made the comment that I liked the key chain. I also added that I was intrigued by the life of Che, so later he gave me the old key chain as a gift. Then he went into his room and brought me back a book. It was a publication of Che's diary when he was in Bolivia. I did not really know what to say, which is unusual for me, as I love to talk. Still, I managed to mumble something that sounded like *"Gracias."* I was taken aback by their hospitality, their honesty, and their generosity. It was interesting that a family who had very little were so willing to give me gifts. It's that type of unrelenting generosity that continues to set the Latino culture apart from the American culture. Compared with the rest of the world, we Americans have everything, yet we are some of the most selfish people you will meet.

After dinner, we walked through the dark streets of Jaimanitas until finally arriving at Miriam's house. Miriam is a historian who lives in the community, and she was waiting for me to arrive so that she could shower me with knowledge about her community and her Cuba. The conversation with Miriam the Historian was about the history of Jaimanitas and other topics related to Cuba. This was extremely educational because Miriam was full of information related to Cuban philosophy, art, history, and politics. She was extremely well-educated and had her master's degree in Cuban art and culture. She was excited to talk to me about her town, Jaimanitas, which has historically been a fishing town. Interestingly enough, this humble little fishing town is adjacent to the current residence of the president, who lives no more than three to five miles away in Miramar. Miramar is home to many of the embassies in Cuba and was once the community where many of the rich Cubans lived before the revolution. Of course Fidel Castro's house is not easily accessible, as you would have to pass through countless checkpoints as well as past multiple military personnel before ultimately arriving. Although Fidel's house is set back and a bit guarded, when he used to be healthy, the people from the local community would see him out and about, jogging through the community of Miramar. However, now that he is not in good health, very few people see Fidel, as he makes very few, if any, public appearances.

We spent over an hour with Miriam talking about the history of Jaimanitas, the Cuban Revolution, religion, and other interesting topics. Actually, it was more of a lecture from her, and as I listened, I was totally captivated by this intelligent woman. Apparently, even though she was formally educated in art and culture, more or less as a historian, she found herself working with young kids for a time; yet, she does not regret that in the least. Everything for her is a valuable learning experience. This whole conversation took place at the front gate rather than in her home because her house had been demolished, and she was in the process of renovating her home. Apparently, it was one of the last remaining wood houses from the 1940s. According to her, it was time to upgrade. Jaimanitas has historically been a place where fishermen came to rent a house and fish. And the wooden houses were the last true memory of that era. Perhaps that was why she had held out as long as she had.

The other thing that I found interesting during our conversation was that she not only had a master's degree, but that it didn't cost her any money to earn it. In other words, she received all of her school courtesy of the State, which, according to what I came to find out, wasn't unique. Here in Cuba, K-12 as well as higher education, is free for everyone. Personally, I found that to be a positive attribute of the Cuban socialist system. Any Cuban who chooses to seek out an education, even a post-bachelor's degree, is able to do that, free of charge. So I asked her why she didn't continue to get her PhD if it was free of charge; however, she told me that she had to take care of her mother and tend to other family issues. So she had to temporarily suspend her pursuit of a PhD. Miriam, by the way, is in her late fifties and is still an eager learner, which is inspiring to me. The interesting irony of the "free school" scenario is that, although they can study for free, in many cases, they lack the proper implements to take advantage of this. For example, Miriam did not own a computer when she was getting her MA degree, and furthermore, she had trouble getting access to a computer to do her coursework, which made it pretty hard to turn in assignments or even do research. She was able to do the bulk of her research at the national library and other institutions that had accessible archives for research. While that particular challenge could be resolved, it is quite peculiar that, although an individual is free to study at no cost—provided you have the intellectual capacity to maintain good grades—they still lack the basic implements with which to study. I found that to be quite interesting, as it is indicative of what Cuba has suffered as a result of the U.S.-imposed trade embargo.

Our conversation was very interesting and informative. It allowed me to get a really objective opinion about Cuban history. She asked me if I had any questions, and even though I did, I told her that I felt like some of them may be offensive to the current government. Nevertheless, she quickly replied that it is "okay to ask those questions," because even though that type of behavior was extremely forbidden historically, now there is more dialogue about the government and the revolution itself. Furthermore, she added, "There are good things and bad things about all governments because they are run by human beings. And human beings, by our very nature, are imperfect." Still, I chose to hold my tongue.

LA PLAZA DE LA REVOLUCIÓN AND MORE

I was finally able to visit the *Plaza de la Revolución* and see where all of the historical speeches given by Fidel Castro took place, at least the speeches given in Havana, Cuba. In *La Plaza de la Revolución*, one can find all of the government buildings, including the presidential building, which is on the other side of the street from the plaza, as well as the monument to José Martí.

While Martí was certainly a revolutionary, he was not a born combatant. Sadly, one of the main reasons that Martí chose to fight in the war against Spain was because many people criticized him for instigating the war, but not *fighting* in it. So in order to prove himself, he joined the war and was killed shortly thereafter. José Martí was an intellectual and a writer. His sojourns to the United States and other parts of Latin America were both inspirational as well as motivational, and served as ways to raise money for the Cuban War of Independence. In my opinion, he had no need to prove himself, as he had already done that by doing what he did best, which was using his pen and his voice to "fight" for independence. Now, the giant obelisk and statue of José Martí that adorn the plaza and stand behind Castro as he speaks to the Cuban people is there to remind everyone of the vital role he played in Cuba's gaining her independence from Spain.

Additionally, two more of the most important figures of the Cuban Revolution, Che Guevara and Camilo Cienfuegos, adorn the government buildings that face outward into the plaza. Anyone who attended one of Fidel's speeches stood in the middle, surrounded by some of Cuba's most powerful icons. Meanwhile, just on the other side of the plaza is the presidential building where the president and the executive members work.

Che Guevara and Camilo Cienfuegos were two extremely different personalities; still, both were instrumental in the Cuban Revolution. Unfortunately they both died shortly after the Revolution. Che was killed in Bolivia trying to carry out a Cuban-like revolution in the mountains of Bolivia, and Camilo was tragically killed in a plane crash. But their images still live on and adorn buildings, murals, and shirts, and their images are sought after by tourists from around the world who come to learn about Cuba, its revolution, its culture, and its history.

Of course, not every Cuban in Cuba, or in other parts of the world, would consider Fidel and his revolutionaries heroes, as many are not content with the current state of the union. In fact, now that there is a bit more freedom of speech in Cuba, some of the Cuban people are beginning to open up and share their unhappiness with many of the tourists. For instance, as I was riding in a taxi, I told the taxi driver that "I could live in Cuba," and he quickly replied to me and said, "You say that because you don't live here." So even though approximately 60 percent of the Cuban people are satisfied with their government—a statistic provided to me by numerous Cubans—there is still 40 percent of the population who want to see things change.

I spoke with another taxi driver who was a retired government engineer. He told me about the Special Period, which started in 1991, following the collapse of the USSR. During that time, the USSR ceased to exist as the Soviet Union, and Cuba went into an economic freefall, and people had to ration everything carefully. Before that, he was earning seven hundred and fifty Cuban pesos (approximately $200) a month, which made for a pretty good retirement. This was before the new Cuban currency (the CUC) was introduced to the Cuban economy. However, during the Special Period, that retirement salary was reduced to the equivalent of $11 a month. Granted, his house and health care were taken care of by the government; nonetheless, this was a tough time for him, as he had to try and live off that $11 per month.

According to him, once an individual went to the *tienda* (a small store that sells basic food items) twice, he or she had used up all of the available money for the month. This was not only a hard time for this retired gentleman, but it was a tough time for all Cubans, as the USSR, who was their biggest financial sponsor, crumbled and could barely take care of its own people. They left Cuba to fend for itself, a decision that almost led to Cuba's demise.

To make matters worse for the Cuban people, it was illegal to be caught with foreign currency such as dollars, pounds from England, pesetas from Spain, francs from Switzerland or France, or any other foreign currency, and this was punishable with up to a year in jail. This made it even more difficult for the local Cubans to survive on a month-to-month basis. It is hard to blame the Cuban government because they themselves were suffering from budget cuts as well, and were struggling to take care of their own people and still hold strong to their socialist practices. Therefore, the society as a whole had to make major adjustments to their lifestyle. So as a result, not everyone empathizes with the revolution. Many people lost everything as a result, and had to leave the country with only the clothes on their backs.

However, before one begins to compare Cuba with the United States, it would be better to first assess each country's political and economic system within their own countries. Or, as I have already discussed, compare each country with similar countries, in terms of the progress of their development. That is, compare Cuba to developing countries, and compare the U.S. to developed countries, not to each other. Only then could one theoretically begin to compare these two nations on a country-to-country level. Because to compare the USA to Cuba is like comparing a lobster dinner to a steak dinner. You must first compare the meals individually in order to see if the steak, as a steak, is cooked to your liking. And similarly, you have to make sure that the lobster, as a lobster, is cooked as a lobster should be. Then, and only then, can you say which plate fits your personal preference.

Cuba, after the revolution, is a country that was built primarily on Marxist principles, and would therefore be considered a communist country. In Cuba, you see more socialist-based rhetoric and propaganda in their graffiti and on their billboards, which is something that will be discussed in more depth in a subsequent chapter. For the sake of this book, however, I will refer to Cuba as a socialist state run by the Communist Party of Cuba. They were officially calling themselves a Marxist-Leninist state, politically and economically speaking, up until the Special Period. Subsequently, they have dropped that label. Still, the system's foundation is built upon these schools of thought, and has since been molded into what one sees in modern-day Cuba.

Additionally, one must acknowledge the integration of Che Guevara's idea of the *new man*. It could be argued that after Che's departure and subsequent death, this idea became less prevalent, as it was Che who was the primary promoter of this ideology. The concept of the "new man" assumes that all humans are so passionate about helping one another that they are willing to work all day, not only for themselves, but also for the betterment of the society in which they live. In other words, this concept, which is Marxist in theory, relies on the idea of altruism as the basis for building a utopian society.

Unfortunately, this theory never truly came to fruition because there were too many people who were not interested in "working to better the society." In fact, some Cubans have made the assertion that Fidel politely "excused" Che from Cuba because of a difference in ideology and overall vision for Cuba. Others believe that the reason was Che's openly critical speech about the Soviet Union in 1965 in Algeria. This speech enraged the Soviet Union, who at the time, was helping Cuba with both weapons and money. Upon Che's return to Cuba, after speaking in Africa, he and Fidel met secretly, which many suggest led to Che's departure for the Congo to fight in the liberation movement shortly thereafter. In fact, it would seem to be more like a savvy political move by Fidel in order to not lose the support of the Soviet Union, than a simple disagreement in ideologies; however, this assertion is still speculation, as no one really knows what was said in the secret meeting between Fidel and Che. Whatever the truth of the matter, the Marxist mentality itself still permeates most of Cuba's political thought and economic policies.

Within Cuba, all of the members of the society have access to a defined set of basic rights. This is one of the positive attributes of a fully socialized society: the basic right to health care and education. The only problem is that even though they all have access to these basic human rights, there is a lack of resources such as school supplies and medicine. In other words, if you are sick and need to go to the doctor, it's free of charge. In fact, the doctor will even write you a prescription to be filled, often free of charge.[21] But the likelihood of that medicine being at the pharmacy is precarious (or perhaps is being sold in CUC, which would make it unaffordable for the patient). I was told that sometimes, if the patient has a severe injury or diagnosis, and the medicine is not available, the doctor will prescribe him or her with something else that will "ease the pain," and for lack of a better term, send them to the afterlife with a smile on his or her face. Of course this is not often the case, as Cuba is known for its skilled doctors and nurses. Cuba has even sent highly qualified doctors to all parts of the developing world as a courtesy from the Cuban government. This is an extremely humanitarian act, and it also shows the level of professionalism of the Cuban doctors.

With regard to education, many of the schools are lacking basic supplies such as pencils, pens, and notebooks. This is not to say that no one has these materials; rather, they are not abundant. Even at the university level, many people lack some of the basic items to type a paper or do research. I have already discussed this in an earlier chapter. Yet, it is worth noting that not having these items does not keep people from pursuing these degrees; it merely makes it a bit more challenging.

Salaries are not very high in Cuba because the State is responsible for paying everyone, and unfortunately, Cuba's economy is not doing well. Moreover, *el bloqueo* prohibits U.S.-Cuban relations on an international business level (not to mention political and economic as well), unless you are one of many right-wing Cuban-Americans who are benefiting from the embargo. This is another reason why these people are lobbying to keep the embargo in place—they are actually benefiting from it financially.

These Cuban-Americans are the ones, in many cases, who run the businesses back in the U.S. that facilitate travel back and forth to Cuba. In other words, and despite the irony, many of these individuals own Cuban travel agencies and shipping companies that focus on sending money, goods, and services to Cuba. The embargo is beneficial to them because it provides job security. Without the embargo, there would be less of a "monopoly," as many of these businesses would either cease to exist or have more competition. In fact, there are some who go to

Cuba and fund their entire trip by bringing back and selling Cuban cigars to their friends back here in the U.S. Ironically, many of these individuals who staunchly support the embargo have family who still live in Cuba, and continue to suffer under *el bloqueo*; nevertheless, they continue to perpetuate this self-serving way of thinking. On the other hand, other Cuban-Americans and their right-wing political constituents in the U.S. continue to support the embargo because they see it as a way to make Fidel pay for "ruining" their country, and subsequently "forcing" them to leave their country of birth.

This kind of business does not contribute to perpetuating the Cuban state or sustaining the internal traditional economy. Therefore, because of the poor Cuban economy (which has recently begun to open its doors to tourism), the government is only able to give so much to each person. In regard to the salaries themselves, they are extremely low in comparison to other countries in the developing world; however, the major difference is that Cuba, unlike most other developing nations, guarantees citizens a free education, free health care, inexpensive (or free) rent, and inexpensive water and electric bills. So the $50 a doctor makes each month by no means allows him or her to save, but does help to buy more food or other items.

On the other hand, looking at a country such as Guatemala, the average worker earns approximately $300 per month, but still has to buy food for the whole family, live in a relatively poorly built house, have little to no access to good medical facilities or even doctors or nurses, study at a substandard school because they can't afford $200 a month for private school, and so on. Comparing Cuba against its nation-colleagues, it is possible to say, perhaps, that Cubans are living a better quality of life. One can't say that Cubans live better than everyone; but perhaps one can if comparing the sociopolitical ideology and way of life of Cuba with other countries in the developing south (a geographical description including the countries in Latin America, Africa, and Asia that are underdeveloped).

As I have already mentioned, the Cuban system is built on Marxist-Leninist ideas as well as the revolution's ideology of creating the "new man." Che wanted to create a society, utopian in nature, where people lived and worked harmoniously and altruistically and were unconcerned with making personal capitalist gains. Rather, people would work together to build a better society. When Che was given the role of President of the Bank of Cuba, he instituted a maximum salary, which was so low that many of the workers quit. Some of them left and went to the U.S. to seek asylum and find work. So the assumption that everyone will work altruistically for the greater good of a society seemed to be even too idealistic for some of Che's revolutionary *compañeros*. In other words, this ideology sounds great in theory; but it leaves out two basic, yet extremely important, intrinsic components of human nature: greed and the drive to outdo one another for capital gain.

In a true Marxist-Leninist economy, the concept of upward mobility in terms of financial gain is essentially viewed as frivolous (unless you are the State). In Cuba, a doctor still makes more than a janitor. It's just not that big of a difference. And a janitor makes more than someone who chooses not to work. That makes the difference between the incomes of the doctor and the non-worker only $30 a month.

This is an extremely provocative concept, and it was interesting to see it played out in Cuba. Personally, I think the Marxist-Leninist approach could work if Cuba had a stronger economy and something that they could export (other than good doctors) and that could raise their GDP. Then spreading the wealth, which they would actually have, would be much easier. In short, the concept behind Cuba's system is so contrary to everything that I have grown up with in capitalist USA, that I have had to work hard to do away with any preconceived notions—or anti-Cuba rhetoric—that I have been taught growing up. That has been a challenging obstacle to overcome. Nevertheless, it is mandatory if I am going to truly assess the Cuban system and give it the credit it deserves.

EXPLORING THE COUNTRYSIDE OF VIÑALES

Viñales is one of those places where you go to completely forget about the rest of the world. It is only about two hours west of Havana in the province of Pinar del Río. It is famous for its beautiful mountains, its rock structures (which lend itself to some of the best rock climbing in the Western Hemisphere), and alluring hidden caves. It is a place that is quiet and tranquil and where many of the people get around by horseback and work the fields, farming rice, yucca, and tobacco.

I had heard about the tobacco farmers and the interesting rock cliffs, so as soon as I arrived at Viñales and was greeted by Carla and taken to my *casa particular,* I immediately asked how I could find someone to take me on horseback through the mountains to see all of these amazing sites up close and personal. Of course, Carla was not going to let me out of the house to go horseback riding without making me a proper lunch. And when I say "proper," I mean rice, beans, fresh veggies, fresh fruit, and freshly made mango juice to wash it all down.

After filling up on more food than I should have eaten, I took off for the mountains. One of Carla's friends took me to meet Miguel, my guide, who already had our two horses prepped and ready to go. And off we went into the mountains. As I rode on horseback through these trails, all I could think about was how beautiful the scenery was and how majestic this place was. I felt like part of some old film that was based in the Cuban countryside. We were in no rush, and it seemed that the horses weren't either, as we traversed the countryside at an extremely slow pace. That was fine with me, because I really don't like horseback riding, especially when they start trotting or running. I find it extremely uncomfortable when they start to trot, gallop, or go any faster than a stroll, maybe because I am not a natural horseman. This leisurely pace was ideal for me. Another advantage was that I could carry my camera in my hand fairly easily and take pictures at will.

We made our way up into the mountains and made what I expected would be a quick stop at Miguel's friend's house. He had suggested stopping there because his friend was a tobacco farmer and he could show me how they made cigars. I had been expecting some sort of tobacco farming production, or something a bit more official-looking; however, that was just my own lack of knowledge of how the cigar-making process works. After visiting for a little while and talking about Cuba, the USA, and life in general, I asked him about the cigars. Although I do not smoke, I was curious to learn how a real Cuban cigar is rolled from scratch.

Miguel's friend left for a minute then came back with a couple of dry tobacco leaves in his hand and several tools. Luckily, I remembered to grab my video camera and film the rolling process before it was too late. As I was filming, he laid out about three pieces of tobacco—three dried tobacco leaves—rolled them up, cut one of the ends, then added another small piece of tobacco to go over top of the already rolled cigar. After sealing it with fresh honey, he cut the other end off. And *voila*, there was a cigar, ready to be smoked. After hanging out for a bit longer and reveling in the picturesque landscape, Miguel and I headed off to check out some of the caves that were nearby.

We went to a cave called the Cave of the Golondrinas, or *Cueva de las Golondrinas* in Spanish. A *golondrina* is the name of the bird that lives in this particular cave. Well, at least they lived at the entrance—bats live a little farther inside. It was a beautiful little cave that had water droplets falling from above. And that, along with the interesting rock structures and the sunbeams making their way into the cave, created a very serene and tranquil ambiance. I could clearly imagine some of the Tainos, the indigenous group from this part of the Caribbean, hiding away in there to get away from the sun or to have some sort of spiritual retreat or ceremony. I am sure that it was an amazing getaway for them; however, I doubt that it is as habitable during the rainy season.

We were fortunate that it was not raining, nor was it flooded, and so we decided to descend into the cave to have a look. After walking around for a while and taking a few pictures, we decided that it was time to make our way back home. The return route took us through some of the most picturesque parts of the entire excursion. We made our way through streams of running water, valleys of yucca, or cassava, plants that were surrounded by giant rock outcroppings, and finally arrived back at the horse stable. It was, no doubt, one of the most interesting experiences that I had in Cuba up until this point of my trip. It was entirely different from anything I had done since I arrived. And to be able to go around the countryside on horseback, just as the local people do, made it that much more unique and authentic.

The next day, I met up with my host's friend, Mario, and he took me rock climbing on some of the cliffs in the national park. The interesting thing about rock climbing here is that even though it is growing in popularity extremely quickly among locals who have picked up the sport, as well as among international rock climbers who come here specifically to take advantage of some of the best rock climbing in the Western Hemisphere, it is not exactly *legal* to rock climb in the national park. While it is not technically considered *illegal*, if a park guard finds people rock climbing, he or she asks them to leave. Perhaps the government views these types of activities as vandalizing the natural landscape. Despite this, my friend Mario and his friends have been petitioning the government to allow them to open a rock climbing business so that they can be an official association, and thus take international climbers on legal climbing expeditions.

This does not stop them from taking people climbing in the parks and other places in and around Viñales. They also have their unofficial rock climbing group with a president and everything else official. All of their equipment is donated to them by international climbers who go hiking with Mario and his friends and, at the end of their time climbing in Viñales, leave behind some of their equipment. And with that, Mario and his group have been able to piece together some top-quality professional climbing gear.

After breakfast, I walked with Mario to the national park to see a place that Mario wanted to take me to. I told him that I had never officially rock climbed outdoors; I had only climbed before at an indoor rock climbing gym in the USA. While there are some similarities, recreational indoor climbing is nothing like the *real* thing. So I told Mario that I wanted to go somewhere that was better set up for beginner- to intermediate-level climbers. In order to honor my request, Mario picked out a place in the national park, but before we could enter the park, one of Mario's friends stopped us to say that the *inspectors* were there walking around. An inspector is different from a park guard. An inspector is a government-hired worker who comes around to make sure that people are not doing any illegal activities pertaining to tourism. For example, the inspectors would stop someone who is illegally renting horses to tourists, or illegally hosting tourists, among other things. Their job is to make sure no one is doing anything on the black market. And even though we were not doing anything that could be deemed illegal in the technical sense, we decided that it was still better to not challenge anyone. So we continued down another path that would take us away from the inspectors and that would lead us to another place that Mario knew, which was still inside the park. However, as we were walking to the other destination, one of the park guards was there monitoring the vicinity. So we acted as though we were going somewhere else and just kept walking.

After walking a bit more through the middle of the countryside, where I had, coincidentally, been horseback riding the day before, we decided to go to yet another place, which, according to Mario, is never visited by any of the inspectors or the park guards. In fact, this place was quite spectacular, and I was wondering why we just didn't go straight there in the first place. For me, it was perfect. It was a rock outcropping that consisted of about three or four large monolithic structures that formed a natural cave. The other great thing about this place was that we were not out in the blazing sun trying to climb; instead, we could be inside this natural rock outcropping, in the shade. Moreover, since it was a place that no one visits, it was extraordinarily peaceful and breathtaking. This Plan C worked out well, and we were able to spend the next four hours rock climbing out in the middle of nowhere. We would probably have stayed out longer, but after climbing for that long, my arms felt like they were going to explode from all the pulling and grabbing. This is probably because I had not yet built up those all-important rock-climbing muscles. Nevertheless, it was amazing to be thirty to forty feet in the air scrambling up rocks. Once I got high enough, I was able to peek out over the trees and get a great panoramic view of the countryside of Viñales. It was a fantastic adventure, and Mario was an excellent guide. He taught me how to use the ropes and other equipment associated with climbing, which was important since I knew very little about proper climbing techniques like belaying, rappelling, and so on. It was also comforting to know that when I was thirty to forty feet in the air and unable to hold on to the wall, I could let go of the wall and swing a bit in order to rest my arms, because I knew that Mario was a trustworthy climbing partner.

After climbing, I was able to go home to relax and get things ready for the next leg of my trip, which was to go back to Havana to meet up with a few friends. While I was relaxing at Carla's house, she brought me a book that she had read called *Heaven Is For Real*, by Todd Burpo and Lynn Vincent, about a little boy who claimed to have experienced heaven during a near-death experience. She was naturally reading the Spanish version, which had been left behind by someone else who had stayed at her *casa*. That sparked an interesting conversation about Cuba and religion, during which I asked her about how free Cubans are to practice a formal religion.

To give a little history of religious freedom in Cuba: there was a time when Cuba was considered non-religious, and persecuted anyone who was openly practicing his or her faith. Up until the early 1990s, before the fall of the Soviet Union, and when Cuba declared itself a Marxist-Leninist state, freedom of religion was nonexistent.[22] It wasn't until the mid-1990s, when Pope John Paul II made a trip to Cuba, that Cuba began to allow its citizens to practice their faith openly. Freedom of religion is still relatively new to many Cubans. Nonetheless, my host just laughed and told me that Cubans are free to practice whatever religion they want. She then pointed to the center of town where a cathedral acts as the centerpiece of the city. She said that they hold mass there regularly, and that even though she was not officially Catholic, both of her sons were baptized in the cathedral, and that her husband attends mass there and owns a Bible. She went on to explain to me that religion is not prohibited there, which seemed in direct contradiction to what the United States' anti-Cuba propaganda had instilled in me all these years.

Instead, it appears that people are free to worship and to claim to be part of any religion they want. Still, it is important to note that I cannot attest to seeing any evidence of any non-Judeo-Christian religions. This is not to say, however, that they don't exist, or are forbidden, in Cuba; only that I did not witness any of these other religious groups in practice.

Carla added that there are plenty of Catholic items in her house, and by no means did she make it sound that they were hard to get; they certainly were not forbidden. The inspectors weren't going to take her to jail for belonging to a particular faith and practicing it openly.

I explained that I had heard that in Cuba, people were not permitted to belong to any religion because that was prohibited in a communist-run country. She responded, "Where did the people who told you this get their information?" She further added that the Jehovah's Witnesses go door to door here, just like they do in just about every other country in the world. Also, there are Adventist churches and other churches in Viñales, which is not a very big town. So the church-per-square-mile ratio seemed to be pretty impressive. Carla did add the caveat that even though some of the smaller cities in Cuba may seem Christian, many of the people in Havana practice *Santeria,* which is a blend of Catholicism and African traditions that began to emerge after the arrival of the African slaves at the beginning of the 16th century. Ultimately, what I took away from this conversation was that everyone is free to be part of whatever religion they choose, and in no way is there any sort of religious oppression being enforced by the government of Cuba. In short, the preconceived notions that I had about Cuba were slowly being proven to be incorrect, which was precisely why I had chosen to travel to this country. Being here helped me to sort through all of the propaganda and see the truth and beauty of a country like Cuba.

While Cuba is by no means free of problems, its sociopolitical system does have positive attributes that successfully provide most Cubans with a dignified quality of life. Naturally, given that it has flaws just like any other system in the world, it leaves room for people to criticize it and highlight these flaws, particularly people living in the USA.

I shared with my climbing partner, Mario, that I was told by a friend that "Cubans are the most oppressed people that he had ever met." Mario just laughed and said, "We are not oppressed." He explained that while their system is certainly not perfect, a large majority of the people are content with the government. His only major complaint was that he couldn't get his rock climbing business approved. That had him a bit frustrated, and for good reason: he had a great idea that would mutually benefit him and his friends, the international climbers, and of course, the Cuban government, as they would undoubtedly take the largest percentage of the profits. But all in all, he certainly wouldn't define himself, his friends, or his community, as oppressed.

However, just as I thought that I was getting a clearer understanding of the Cuban mindset, I met someone who totally threw my analysis for a loop. That person was my friend Ryan. I met him one night while I was in Viñales. While we were hanging out, we started to talk a bit about Cuba and its economic and political situation. I opened the subject by saying that if the Cuban government would allocate some funds to painting Havana's dilapidated buildings, then it would be one of the most beautiful cities that I have ever seen. The buildings in Havana are extremely beautiful and hold so much history inside their walls; however, there has been hardly any attempt to maintain or restore them. Even a fresh coat of paint would give them a more aesthetic appeal. Havana is full of European architecture, beautiful plazas, and impressive statues; however, much of it is dilapidated and worn down, and as a result, some of its appeal and beauty are lost. There are a few places in Havana that have been restored, such as parts of Old Havana and the plazas in that area. Most notably, the *Plaza de Armas* and adjacent plazas were restored after being declared a UNESCO World Heritage Site in 1982, and now provide people with phenomenal *avenidas* on which to explore and appreciate the old city.

Ryan told me that there are sufficient funds for this; however, it seems that those funds are allocated to other things, such as the president's salary, who, he said, makes more than a staggering $100,000,000 annually. Compared to average Cubans, including doctors, who make approximately $50 a month ($600 annually), that seems to be a bit ironic, given that one of the purposes of the revolution was to provide everyone with a sense of equality. Perhaps "sense" is the operative word in this case. In general, I would not consider Ryan someone who sympathizes with the revolution, as he was a bit critical of the current government. To change the subject a bit, I told him that in the United States, there are many of the same concerns, but they are manifested differently. The other thing that I found to be interesting was that the word "capitalist" is a bad word in Cuba, much like "communist" and "socialist" are bad words in the United States. It would seem a bit logical that these opposing ideologies would find the words describing their economic and political nemeses to have undesirable connotations, and therefore to invoke a certain negative imagery when used. Personally, as an ethnographer, I try to look past this and try to see the good and bad in both.

After talking a bit about these sensitive and politically loaded themes, we had a bit of a laugh about the Internet here in Cuba. Ryan asked me, "Do you know why the Internet is so expensive and slow, and therefore, nearly impossible for the average local to access?" Of course I already knew the reason behind it—censorship—so I just nodded my head and said yes. Ryan told me that another thing that was censored in Cuba was access to American sports TV shows, especially Major League Baseball. Although channels such as CNN and ESPN were shown in the airports and in the state-run hotels, those were not part of the standard, state-run TV programming that the general public gets to watch. This is done, according to Ryan, so that the Cuban people cannot see some of their former countrymen playing there and earning millions of dollars. In fact, I was told that it is illegal for any athlete to leave Cuba and play in any other country. So the only way to make it to countries such as the United States is to go there illegally, be it via raft, boat, or immigrating into the United States from another country, such as Mexico or Canada.

Cuban athletes are allowed to leave the country to compete; still, they are forbidden to leave to play professionally in other countries. Unfortunately, I was unable to adequately investigate this assertion. Nevertheless, what sometimes happens in these cases is that when a particular team, baseball, soccer, track and field, or any other, is playing in another country, some of the individuals choose to defect, or just stay in that country and either play there, or make their way to the

United States to try to make it big in the major leagues. These athletes do not come back because they can make millions of dollars in other countries as professional athletes, whereas in Cuba, they only earn about \$100–\$150 a month and live a relatively humble existence. Of course, they are still seen as "famous athletes," yet their salary does not compare to the salary of a famous athlete in other countries. Thus, the temptation to defect is extremely strong.

It was lucky for us that it was a noisy place where we were talking, and I was able to hear Ryan's opinion. And I was happy he shared it with me, even though it was a bit nerve-racking at times, thinking someone could just denounce him for what he was saying. That appears to be a pervasive fear among many Cubans; however, I had also heard from other Cubans that the Cuban people are free to talk about their likes and dislikes regarding the Cuban government. As far as where the line is drawn, I am not quite sure. We did not have the misfortune to find out that evening either, which was a good thing. Another time, Ryan was not quite so lucky. He told me that one day he was taking a few tourists horseback riding in the mountains of Viñales and he was talking freely about the government to them. A *campesino* on a horse passed them, and as he did, he stopped and told Ryan to watch what he was saying. This *campesino* happened to be an undercover official, and had the man not known Ryan personally, he would have been in a bit of trouble.

JINETERAS AND CUBA'S DOMESTIC BRAIN DRAIN

After leaving Viñales, I had to make a quick stop in Havana to meet my friend Jessika and her medical school friends from Colombia. We all planned to travel east together to Trinidad, Cienfuegos, and Santa Clara. From there, they were heading back west toward Havana, and I would continue to travel east toward Holguín. It would have been easier, logistically speaking, to go straight from Viñales to Cienfuegos; however, I thought it would be more fun to return to Havana for several more nights and pick up a few travel companions. Not to mention that they are all doctors, so I figured that I would be in good hands if anything happened to me during our travels together.

I had never met Jessika in person. We met through a travel website called Couch Surfers (www.couchsurfing.com). She was going to be in Cuba, and was asking for information about the place, and I sent her a link that I had read from a fellow Couch Surfer. Then we realized that we were all going to be in Cuba around the same time, so we decided to meet in Havana. Taking into account that the Internet and phone communication were both extremely difficult, we set a time to meet at the *Hotel Nacional,* which is not only a landmark in Havana, but also a good place to find people. Its central location between our hotels in Vedado made it easy for us both to walk there and easy to meet up. Of course *easy* is a relative term when you are talking about Cuba, or international travel in general for that matter. Jessika was flying in from

Colombia, and I was taking a bus from Viñales to Havana. Had anything not gone according to plan, we would never have been able to inform one another of the schedule change, and my attempt to meet up with her and her friends would have been wasted. Nevertheless, it was worth the chance, and thankfully for us, it all worked out well.

Jessika showed up at the *Hotel Nacional* about ten minutes after I did. I guess you can say that it was "mission accomplished." Once we had found each other, we went back to my *casa particular* to join some other travelers for dinner and then to go out and see what Havana had to offer us on a Friday night. Our *casa* owners, Andy and Juliet, recommended that we check out *La Casa de la Música,* which is a very famous night spot in Cuba. There are several of them around the country, more or less like a franchise. Ironically, that is not the word used to describe them because that is a capitalist word, and therefore, they do not use those types of words to describe businesses in Cuba.

In any case, there are multiple locations of *La Casa de la Música* that are found in Havana, as well as in other cities in Cuba, so call it what you will. Taking their advice, we took a taxi to *La Casa de la Música* in Miramar. We chose to go to the one in Miramar as opposed to the one in Central Havana because the one in Miramar was said to be better. I am not sure what *La Casa de la Música* was like in Central Havana, but this one was full of *jineteras,* or Cuban women who will "escort" you for a certain fee, and people who apparently go to this type of establishment to look for *jineteras*.[23] Evidently this is a relatively normal phenomenon in Cuba, and so we just ignored it the best we could and tried to enjoy the live salsa music.

One thing that I have noticed in Cuba is that many of the women chose to work as *jineteras* because they can make considerably more money working in that industry, as opposed to getting a more conventional career, and thus contributing to the real Cuban economy. In fact, I would consider this phenomenon as a sort of "domestic brain drain" in that many Cuban citizens choose to work outside the formal infrastructure of the society, and therefore, fail to contribute to the formal local Cuban economy. Let's take these women, for example: instead of working as a nurse, a lawyer, a teacher, etc., they chose to work as an escort and spend their nights looking to get picked up by a lonely tourist. But these *jineteras* will make in one night what a Cuban doctor will earn in two months. And furthermore, earning a doctor's salary, which is approximately $50 a month, is barely enough to live on. So these women leave their formal careers, and in doing so, the formal Cuban infrastructure, and work in the peripheral society that has been created as a result of Cuba's tourism industry. The dichotomy between Cubans and tourists is so extreme that it has created sort of a vacuum effect where many of the professionals, who once contributed to the local Cuban society, are now working informally in the tourism industry and earning significantly more than most people who work and participate in the non-tourist, or traditional, Cuban society.

Another example of this Cuban domestic brain drain is the *casa particular* owners. For example, Andy and Juliet are two extremely educated Cubans (actually most Cubans are well educated) who used to work professional jobs; however, they chose to open a *casa particular* because it earns them more money. As I mentioned previously, Juliet has a graduate degree and used to teach at the University of Havana, Fidel Castro's alma mater, which is arguably the most elite school in Cuba. However, after teaching at the university for over sixteen years, she decided that she would try her luck in the tourism industry, and so she opened a *casa particular,* which she and Andy run. And although it is a lot of work and takes a lot of patience, she makes more money doing that than she ever would have made teaching at the university. I had to ask myself, what incentives do these professionals have to work within the professional infrastructure of Cuba? Of course, many of the *jineteras* were professionals as well, but they realized that working as an escort was much more lucrative. In fact, some of these women who were working as *jineteras* were married and lived lives that one would consider normal, or traditional, according to the established norms of Cuban society. But at night, they get dressed up in provocative clothing and look for a tourist to "take care of " for the night. This, in many cases, is done behind their husband's back.

So one could say that even though the tourism industry in Cuba is very well established and provides a terrific opportunity for tourists to come and see Cuba, it has also created a subculture among the Cubans that is actually detrimental to the socialist infrastructure implemented by the current government. Furthermore, this subculture, operating as it does outside of the regular infrastructure of the society, is counter-productive to the society itself because it is taking professionals away from the formal economy of Cuba. I would predict that if the current socialist system in Cuba stays on the same course for future generations, these subcultures will continue to grow, and the number of professionals in the Cuban society will continue to decrease; and this will be the catalyst that ultimately brings an end to the Cuban socialist system. This is not to say, however, that Cuba's socialist ideologies are not working at all. Quite the contrary; I would say that the socialist infrastructure of Cuba has produced some of the most well-trained and well-educated people in Latin America. However, there need to be a few critical social reforms implemented in order for the revolution's ideology to continue to move forward and adapt to a Cuba that is on the verge of a tourism boom.

DISCOVERING HISTORIC TRINIDAD

Trinidad is a small town that has an old and a new, modern section. It is not a big city, so you can make your way around it in a short period of time. It has two plazas, *La Plaza Céspedes*, which is in the middle of the modern part of Trinidad, and *La Plaza Mayor*, which is in the historical part of Trinidad and is host to *La Casa de la Música* and *La Casa de la Trova*. Both of these are outdoor places where one can sit, have a drink, and listen to music. Most of Trinidad is covered with cobblestone streets, much like Antigua, Guatemala or Granada, Nicaragua, whose cities were also designed by the Spanish and which have managed to keep their colonial look intact over the last four-hundred-plus years. It definitely adds a European touch to the city—although I am sure the shock absorbers on the cars that have to drive here are not as thrilled with these streets as I am! Aside from the cobblestone streets, the city is lined with very colorful colonial-style buildings that are painted in many different colors. Some are blue, others yellow, orange, or light pink.

From *La Plaza Céspedes*, you can take a taxi to *Playa Ancón*. It is a short ride, and it is a beautiful Caribbean beach that is long enough for you to walk and walk until you can't walk anymore. It is on a peninsula, and when I was there, it was not very crowded. That could have been because Trinidad, along with the entire central region in Cuba, had suffered from monsoon-like rains for over three days. As a result, the water was not as crystal clear as it normally is. Undaunted, Jessika, Beticia, Julian, Richard, and I went to find out what *Playa Ancón* had to offer. And even though it was not a classically picturesque Caribbean beach day, we still had a great time walking along the beach and just hanging out. The only downside of the whole beach trip was that we had made a deal with our taxi driver to pick us up at 8:30 p.m.; however, as we were walking to the place where he was supposed to meet us, he was pulling away in the other direction. We tried to flag him down, but to no avail. It wasn't even 8:30 p.m. yet. The strangest part of this was that we hadn't paid him yet for the ride there. We couldn't figure out why he didn't wait. Fortunately for us, there was a hotel nearby, and we had the guard call a taxi for us.

On the way home in the taxi, the driver was explaining to me that there are two different types of taxi systems here in Cuba: the government (or state-run) taxis and the privately-owned taxis. Naturally, there are pros and cons to working with either one. For example, the government-run taxi service gets free gas—approximately nine gallons a month—and other state-mandated perks, but they must work at a fixed rate. On the other hand, the private taxis have to pay for their gas and other amenities, but can negotiate their prices with their clients to some extent. In addition, the private taxis are the ones who work later into the night. There is some competition between these two entities. And to help distinguish between the two, the government gives them different license plates. A yellow license plate is for the private taxis and a blue license plate is for the government-run taxis.

It was interesting to see that Cuba has many different-colored license plates to distinguish between the different entities that drive automobiles. There are different colors for the two taxis (blue and yellow), a color for the military (dark green), a color for government automobiles (black), and there is even a different-colored plate for rental cars (maroon). I found that to be a good way of keeping all of the different automobiles organized.

Since Cuba was in the midst of their World Series, baseball fans were going crazy, wearing their teams' jerseys and other paraphernalia. They even had umbrellas with their teams' logos emblazoned on them. An umbrella is a great item to sell to fans in the Caribbean, because it can rain at any given moment, and the rest of the time it can be used to ward off the burning sun. The Cuban World Series was being played between a team from Havana (Industriales), who are comparable to the New York Yankees in terms of their winning legacy, versus a team from Ciego de Avila (Camaguey) who had never won a World Series. At this point, the series was 3-1, with Ciego de Avila up by two games. Although I would not consider myself a huge fan of baseball, I was fortunate enough to be able to catch a couple of games. Interestingly, I happened to be in the hometown of the winner each time I watched a game. So I had the good luck to experience, firsthand, the baseball fever that goes on in Cuba. It's fun to see people rally so enthusiastically behind a team, and when they win, they go out into the streets and sing, dance, and even play more baseball. Even the fact that it was almost midnight didn't stop these fans from going into the streets to recreate some of the plays that they watched their favorite players make during the game.

This is similar to soccer in other countries of Latin America; however, even though it has been said that soccer is growing in popularity in Fidel's Cuba, baseball is still by far the most popular sport. Very few other Latin American countries have this in common with Cuba—Venezuela, the Dominican Republic, and Nicaragua among them—and yet some of the best Major League Baseball players are from Latin America, as a testament to their talent and dedication.

I was able to watch Camaguey win their game while I was in Trinidad. And although Trinidad is actually located in a different province than Camaguey,[24] the people of Trinidad definitely wanted to see Camaguey win the World Series. After all, *"Ciego,"* as they were commonly called, had never won a World Series, and everyone loves an underdog. So it seemed like most of the country, except for Havana, were rooting for Ciego de Avila. As soon as I arrived at my house in Trinidad and put down my bags, I went into the living room to sit with my hosts to watch the rest of the game. It was a great way to break the ice and meet my host family in Trinidad.

The concept of the *casa particular* is unlike anything I have seen in other parts of Latin America. Cubans should consider exporting this idea to the rest of Latin America. It is similar to a home stay, but it is the only legal way for a non-Cuban to stay with a family in Cuba. You can stay in a *casa particular* for a much lower price and get to experience what it's like to live with a Cuban family from the town where you are traveling. The accommodations are marvelous and the food is outstanding. The closest thing I could compare it to would be a combination of a hostel and a home stay. Of course, there are some that are more like a home stay and others that tend to resemble hostels. Either way, it is a relatively inexpensive way to travel. Another advantage is that the other guests who stay tend to be like-minded travelers, which adds to the overall experience. For me, staying in a *casa particular* has been an enlightening experience, and I was treated like a king. The hospitality was extraordinary, and the food was first class—and cheap! A lobster plate, which included a plate of vegetables, rice, beans, potatoes, a fresh fruit drink, and a relatively large lobster tail, has cost me approximately $8 everywhere I went. At this point, I had traveled from the western tip of the island to central Cuba. And I didn't expect it to vary much more as I continued to travel east to Holguín, my final destination.

The idea of the *casa particular*, for me personally, is a great form of anthrotourism because it gives me a chance to live with local families and get a flavor of the local cuisine. I hope that other places in Latin America—and even the world—will begin to adopt something similar. There are home stays in most places that people can be part of; however, they are generally reserved for people who are staying for long periods of time or who are studying or doing volunteer work in that particular country. The *casa particular*, on the contrary, is set up to host travelers for as little as one night as they pass through town. The only drawback to the system is that it has strict tourism policies in place. Thus, it would require other countries to impose strict policies on where a tourist can stay, which would radically change the dynamics of the tourism industry in most other countries.

In Cuba, a tourist has only two options with regard to lodging: a privately run *casa particular* or a government-run, overpriced hotel. As a tourist, you are not legally allowed to stay anywhere else. In fact, if you do choose to stay somewhere else, your host runs the risk of being denounced by his neighbor and then heavily fined by Cuban Immigration. This strict policy regarding tourism was probably put in place to monitor and control where tourists can stay and what they can see. However, it also protects the *casa* owner, as it assures them that tourists will have only the two options, and therefore, it protects the Cuban business owner. So for any other country even to entertain the option of the *casa particular,* it would require a total restructuring of their policies regarding tourism in their country, which could hurt their economy. In short, the idea of the *casa particular* is a unique idea that is exclusive to Cuba's tourism industry, and it may not even be possible to work in other countries around the world simply because the tourists in other countries have a bit more freedom with regard to where they can decide to stay.

As I have traveled across Cuba, I have interviewed people of all different backgrounds and perspectives regarding their particular living situations under the Castro government. The one universal thing that I noticed was that no matter who I talked to or where I traveled, it seemed that the general populace's needs were met at a basic level, unlike in many other countries in the developing world. In fact, one of the interesting things, regarding Cuba as an island nation, is that it has little or no natural resources. Instead, unlike many other developing countries across the developing south, they export professionals—for instance, doctors and nurses—on a worldwide scale. Many of their doctors do humanitarian work and go on medical missions[25] in other parts of the developing world. In fact, as I previously mentioned, Cuban doctors are currently working in over eighty-three countries around the world.

During my travels, I was fortunate enough to be able to see a large part of Cuba, which provided me with a better perspective on the country as a whole. I not only visited the tourist places, but I also spent significant time in the *campo* and the "non-touristy" places that I visited while traveling across the country.

One of the things that interested me the most was that many of the people that I met lived in houses that were relatively well built in comparison to most of the houses that I have seen in other parts of Latin America. Generally, in Latin America, when you are out in the countryside and away from the formal infrastructure that is found in most cities with their apartment buildings and similar complexes, usually built of concrete and rebar, with a strong foundation, you typically find people making their houses out of wood or other non-durable material. You even see houses made of cardboard boxes and topped with a makeshift roof.

That is not usually the case here in Cuba. In fact, a large majority of the people living out in the rural areas of the Cuban countryside have houses built of brick or concrete. They even have well-built roofs that keep the water out when it rains. In other parts of rural Latin America, many houses look as though they are going to fall over if the wind blows too hard, or they are so porous that there is no way to keep out mosquitos or anything else that decides to fly, walk, or crawl into the house in the middle of the night. This has really impressed me about Cuba's socialist-built infrastructure. It has made an effort to meet the vast majority of the Cuban people's needs. It is important to note that this has been done with no formal U.S. investment or support. I use the term "formal" to refer to the U.S. government's failure to provide economic aid to Cuba as a result of the embargo. However, the remittances from family members living in the U.S. that are sent back to Cuba clearly help to supplement the income of their family members who remain in Cuba. I find this interesting, particularly because the United States claims that their neoliberalist policies are intended to help stimulate economic growth, and therefore, provide their country's citizens with a better sense of upward mobility. This, in turn, should lend itself to a stronger infrastructure, better housing, and so on. Yet, I would go so far as to say that the underprivileged individuals of those countries where the U.S. does provide aid appear to be worse off, in terms of quality of life, than the underprivileged of Cuba.[26] I find that to be quite thought-provoking.

Even though this socialist ideology does, indeed, seek to take care of the majority of the Cuban people, it has its drawbacks, noticeably the lack of incentives it creates for hardworking Cuban professionals. For example, the daughter of the *casa* owner where I stayed was a doctor whose specialty is reading biopsies. And while doctors and professors are some of the highest-paid professionals in Cuba in terms of the State's socialist pay scale that is set by the government, it still only allows them to earn approximately $50 a month. So the daughter worked as a cook and helped her mother with the guests in her *casa* just to make extra money.

Being the owner of a *casa particular* is a lucrative business, especially since the tourism industry has been growing exponentially over the last twenty years. The disadvantage to this is that her granddaughter, who is in her second year at the university, told her mom that she doesn't see the point in studying when she can make more money working as a maid for her grandmother. Nevertheless, her grandmother encourages her to keep studying, because even though that is the way the system is structured now, it may change in the future. So for now, she is staying in school and seeking a college degree like her mother and father, who are both doctors, even though it does not lend itself to making a lot of money in Cuba.

After walking around Trinidad for a day and getting to know this beautiful colonial town, Jessika, Julian, Beticia, Richard and I found out that there were two waterfalls close to the town. One of them was extremely close to town—fifteen minutes by taxi—and the other one was about forty-five minutes away. Since they were both so close, we decided that we were going to visit them. We were told that the one that was farther away, *El Tope de Collantes,* was more spectacular; however, the hiking involved was a bit strenuous for someone who is not in particularly good physical condition. You have to traverse rocks and rivers, climb down slippery rock and mud steps, and do all this in the heat and humidity, which is tough enough for visitors to get used to, particularly travelers who are not accustomed to the tropics. It was going to be a difficult forty-five-minute hike down the mountain to reach the waterfall.

El Cubano, which was the other waterfall, was closer, but when we went there, they told us that it was closed because the bridges that take visitors across some of the rivers were washed away by the heavy rain that passed over central Cuba a couple days before we arrived. In fact, we had been a bit concerned that they would have to suspend our trip if it was still going to be raining the day we wanted to go to Trinidad. However, the rains and raging waters subsided, and we were able to get there safe and sound.

Since *El Cubano* was closed, we decided to go to *El Tope de Collantes* to hike down to the waterfall. I was secretly pleased, because that was the one I had wanted to see all along. The only reason that we were debating it was because the taxi ride was $50, but dividing that by five people made it affordable. It was well worth the investment. The trek down to the waterfall was absolutely breathtaking. The area was full of wildlife, and we spotted numerous birds, snakes, and other creatures right there on the path itself. To our delight, one part of the trail even had a small, rocky, cave-like structure with stalactites. We hiked for forty-five minutes straight down the face of the mountain. I could only assume it was the face, because we were in the middle of the jungle, and I couldn't see our surroundings unless there was a break in the foliage. We could hear the raging water of the waterfall the whole way down, so we knew we were getting close when it got louder and louder until, finally, we arrived at the waterfall.

It was spectacular, as the raging water rushed through a cut-out in the mountainside that looked more like a natural slide than a waterfall. As the water made its way through the winding course it had cut through the mountain over the course of its life, it blasted out into a plunge pool that overflowed into a small stream that continued on its way down the mountain. The only downside to this waterfall was that the water was a bit cold for my taste; however, after that hike, it was refreshing to jump into the water and swim in the plunge pool. As I sat there on a rock in the middle of the pool, I couldn't help but think about the uphill trek that awaited us. Nevertheless, I didn't let it ruin the relaxing moment I had sitting there on the rock. It was as if I were on an island in the middle of nowhere. For a long time, I just stared up into the clear blue sky, daydreaming and watching the swallows play in the mist that came from the waterfall itself. It is one of those moments that makes you feel as if you are in a movie, and sometimes it is hard not to take it for granted. Sometimes, it's only after you get back home and look at the pictures that you realize how special a moment like that was. So in order to try not to miss the moment, I just lay there and tried to soak it in the best that I could—still trying not to think about the uphill battle that was waiting for me.

Although going back up was much more difficult because of the steepness of the climb, I didn't find it to be impossible. Rather, I saw it as a good workout. On the other hand, it was a good thing that we left when we did, because on our way up, we ran into a seventy-three-year-old British man who was having trouble getting up. It was a bit of a challenge for him, and his body was not quite up to the task. German, his Argentine friend who was there at the waterfall with him, had left him to go up and have someone send a horse or someone down to help him. He clearly wasn't going to make it without help. So Jessika, Beticia, and I stopped and helped him and gave him water. I had some vitamin water left in my bottle, which I gave to him with the hope that it would help him regain some sort of strength, because we were still an hour away from the top at a brisk walking pace.

All in all, he was pretty fortunate to run into us, given the fact that Jessika is a doctor. Apparently he had been praying for an angel to come and help him. And though by no means do I see myself as an angel, I was very happy to have been able to help him. He could have been my grandfather, my father, or some other family member. And if I am willing to do that for a family member, why would I not be willing to do that for any other fellow human being who is in trouble? In my mind, a person in need is a person in need, be it a member of my immediate family or a seventy-three-year-old stranger who is on the verge of collapse in the middle of the jungle.

He was going so slowly that we had to stop with him every fifty yards or so to let him recuperate and get his breathing back to normal. He may even have been getting a bit delirious, because when he would sit down, he would begin to tell us random stories about being back in England. He even took out his camera to show us photos of a wedding that he attended back in England. One time when he stopped, he sat down only about two feet from a snake that was coiled up by the side of a tree. He would have never even seen it had Jessika not wanted to try to poke it with her walking stick. I told her I didn't think that would be the best idea since it was happy where it was, and it was a bad idea to annoy it. Instead of being frightened by the snake, the elderly man actually stayed there, took out his camera, and took a picture. That was the moment when I looked at Jessika and told her that he was not doing well. It might have been different had he been someone who was used to the jungle and its inhabitants. However, this guy was from England and was not accustomed to this type of extreme wildlife. So the fact that he was so casual about the snake that was parked next to him was a good indication of his mental and physical condition, which were deteriorating rapidly.

Finally, seemingly out of nowhere, a man on a horse came, and we stopped him to see if he could take this gentleman up to meet his friend. He told us that he had come down for exactly this reason. This came as a huge relief to Jessika and me, as we were a bit concerned that we were going to end up carrying the old man out of the jungle, because there was no way that we were going to leave him there to spend the night by the side of the trail, waiting to be rescued. In his condition, had he attempted to spend the night, he probably would have wandered off into the thick jungle, never to be found again.

The incident with the old man certainly added a bit of excitement to an already-adventurous day. I was thankful that we were able to help this fellow traveler and make sure he got back to his *casa particular* safe and sound. In fact, later that night, we ran into his companion, German from Argentina, who had gone ahead and sent the horse down to rescue our British acquaintance, and he told us that once his English friend got home and was able to lie down and rehydrate, he was fine. It was nice to know that this story had a happy ending.

VISITING CHE IN SANTA CLARA

Leaving Trinidad was tough because I had become pretty close with my host family. Even though I was only there for a total of three days, I was able to really get to know them and their story. They had lived through the revolution and were perfectly happy with the way things are currently going in Cuba. They are by no means well-off monetarily. Nevertheless, they are extremely grateful for everything they have. What was most impressive to me about Cuba was that, at least in theory, no Cuban is going to die of starvation or from lack of medical care. The government is structured in such a way that it provides these essentials to all of its citizens. This is something that distinguishes Cuba from the vast majority of the other developing countries throughout Latin America—as well as most of the developed ones in the hemisphere.

My host family, although they were older, were not concerned with having the proper health insurance, nor did they have to worry whether they were going to eat. Rather, they seemed to enjoy their day-to-day life with the confidence of knowing that those basic needs were taken care of, and should anything happen to them, they will be provided for. When they were talking to me about the street on which they lived, they told me that everybody helps everyone. The exact quote that they said to me was, "We don't divide up the extra, rather, we share what we have." In other words, no one was living a luxurious life monetarily; yet, as a community, they all took care of one another and looked out for each other. If someone were to need something like food, another person would lend it to them. Also, if someone nearby were to get sick in the middle of the night, their daughter, who is a doctor, would happily tend to their needs. And if that required getting them to the hospital, then she would make sure that they got there and were taken care of immediately. My parting could accurately be described as such sweet sorrow, as I took to the road and made my way back through Cienfuegos *en route* to Santa Clara.

Before I left Trinidad, I had already called my next *casa particular* host, José, and reserved my room. I had found out about José through the recommendation of someone who had previously stayed with him. What especially caught my attention was that José had worked as Fidel Castro's chef for forty years. And that was all I needed to know. I figured that if he was good enough to cook for the president of Cuba, then he was definitely more than capable of fixing someone like me a great meal. So I called him from Trinidad and got everything set up. José was even at the bus terminal waiting for me when I arrived, just like my previous hosts had been. That small gesture makes things so much easier when I'm arriving and don't have to figure out where the hosts live and how to get there.

Shortly after my arrival, I knew I had made a great choice by choosing to stay with José and his family. Not only was he a great cook, but, I also came to find out, he was part of the militia in the revolution and fought in the Bay of Pigs invasion. For my purposes, I couldn't have asked for a better person to meet and talk to about Cuba, as José was extremely open and willing to talk about the revolution, his involvement in the Bay of Pigs invasion, his job as a cook, and anything else I thought to ask him. In fact, he said, he made a name for himself as a cook during the Cuban Revolution because he would cook for Fidel Castro and the troops out in the Sierra Maestra Mountains. Apparently, he must have worked miracles out there, because as soon as the revolution ended, he started working in the government as Fidel's chef.

I asked him about Che, Camilo Cienfuegos, Fidel, and Raúl, and he told me that he was part of Camilo's group of fighters, and they were pretty close to him as a friend. In fact, they originally met because he took care of Camilo in Santa Clara when he, Camilo, was staying at one of the hotels. That was the beginning of their relationship as revolutionary *compañeros*. It didn't take long for us to jump right into this conversation—I was eager to ask and he was eager to tell—but before we started "talking revolution," he made us some coffee in the true Cuban fashion. Actually, he made himself a *café cubano* (espresso with sugar), and he made me a *café americano,* and we instantly started talking about the revolution, the leaders of the revolution, and how impressed I was that the revolution is still holding true to most of its ideologies some fifty-three years later. This was especially remarkable because the collapse of the Soviet Union and the subsequent Cuban Special Period almost brought the Cuban economy to its knees.

It was after talking with José for a bit that he told me that he fought at *Playa Girón,* which is the beach next to the *Bahía de Cochinos*—known to us as the Bay of Pigs. That is where the United States launched an attack against Che and Fidel's new government in 1961, shortly after the revolution, using a fighting force of 1,400 American-trained Cuban exiles. This CIA-sponsored attack became known as the Bay of Pigs invasion. The invasion went sadly wrong for the United States when it abandoned soldiers after the initial foray and left them without proper ammunition and reinforcements. This, of course, did not turn out well for those who were involved, as they were not only outnumbered, but outgunned as well, and quickly became prisoners, many of whom were executed in short order. One of the most interesting parts of this conversation was that José told me that when they had these soldiers hostage, the soldiers said to them, "You are Cuban!" as if that was some sort of surprise. The reason for this response was because apparently these "invaders" were told by the United States that the people against whom they would be fighting were Russians and Chinese communists. So naturally, these American-trained fighters were a bit surprised to see that they were fighting against their own countrymen. Unfortunately for these soldiers, neither Che nor Fidel was exactly sympathetic to their rationale or excuses.

What I found really interesting were the similarities between my granddad and José. They are both approximately the same age, both strongly believe in their government, and both were war veterans in their own right. I find it a bit disheartening, though, to think that both of these honorable men would have seen one another as military foes. That is extremely thought-provoking to me because the two of them, if they were to sit down together, would be very similar in just about every way. Yet politically, they were enemies. In my imagination, I could see the two of them sitting together in the plaza, drinking coffee, smoking Cuban cigars (even though my granddad didn't smoke), and exchanging war stories. However, given the time and the politics, instead of hanging out together and talking, they would have been trying to shoot and potentially kill one another. That type of imagery saddens me because these are two principled men who would not only get along extremely well, but would also see eye-to-eye on just about every topic under the sun. During the conversation, I told José that I wished my grandparents had been able to come to Cuba for medical treatments, as they had to pay month after month for doctors' visits, medical procedures, and medications. It is likely that in Cuba, the medical treatment would have been comparable[27] to that in the U.S.; yet, it would have only cost a fraction of what it cost for the equivalent procedure in the U.S.

Since the moment I entered José's house, he was more than willing to share his story with me. And for that, I was grateful. I felt extremely lucky to have met someone who had lived through so much and believed so strongly in Cuba and its revolution. From a socialist perspective, there are many things that Cuba is doing correctly, in trying to take into account the best interests of the Cuban people. I think the problem, in many cases, lies in the implementation of these policies (e.g. having the proper medicines readily available, etc.). Of course the lack of resources is a limiting factor for Cuba, as guaranteeing every citizen health care, education, food, and housing is a tremendous burden to shoulder as a developing country.

One could make the assertion that many of the policies that have been implemented by the State since the triumph of the revolution, have overtly helped to raise the standard of living for most Cubans. The government has also made the conscious effort to provide its citizen with health care and access to free education, irrespective of their socioeconomic status.

I was able to interview various other people in the city of Santa Clara as well, and it seemed that many of them were strongly opposed to the current system in place. One woman that I spoke to said that only about 10 percent of the people were content with the current system as implemented by the government. To ensure that we could continue to talk freely, we went to a place that was extremely noisy so that she could explain to me that, in her opinion, the Cuban people are oppressed because they do not have the freedom to express themselves. And furthermore, she added that if an individual were to openly oppose the current administration, then that person would go to jail. As a foreigner, you are quickly escorted to the airport and expeditiously deported to your country of origin. This particular woman added that if she were to be heard speaking out against the government, then she would run the risk of getting thrown in prison. However, at the same time, and perhaps in a somewhat self-contradictory way, she told me that she is not scared of the government, and when the day comes that she is scared to speak the truth about the system under which she lives, she will find a way to leave the country.

As a follow-up to my conversation with her, I asked her what she thought of Che Guevara, and she said that she actually liked him. I then followed that with a question that I asked many Cubans that I met during my travels, "If Che were alive today, would Cuba be any different?" She told me that she thought that yes, it would be different, and furthermore, it would be better. It was notable that I heard the same sentiment from another person that I interviewed later that same day, discussed below. After asking some general questions about Che and the current governmental system that has been in place for the last fifty-three years, I asked her if she were to have the opportunity to go to the USA and live, would she like to do that? And she told me that historically she would have said no; however, in the recent past, she had been entertaining the thought.

That same day, I had the opportunity to eat lunch at a local *paladar*, which in this case was someone's house where the owners had put up signs advertising the food that they were offering to cook. It happened that this particular *paladar* was near my *casa* where I was staying in Santa Clara. And after checking out the menu, I decided to eat lunch there. How could I refuse? It was a huge lunch with vegetables, fresh mango and guava juice, rice, beans, sweet potatoes, and steak, for $2. That was not an opportunity that I wanted to let slip through my hands. And by no means did I let that happen. In fact, I took full advantage of it and went into their house and sat down with them in the dining room, as if

I were part of their family, and the table was their "restaurant." While I was waiting for them to cook and serve the food, I started talking to them about Santa Clara, Che Guevara, and so on. We then started talking about U.S. and Cuban relations and also about Iraq, among other things. That was when I added the interesting fact that a couple of days ago had been John F. Kennedy's birthday, and I found it ironic that I, a *gringo*, was in Cuba on his birthday. After all, Kennedy was the one who originally put the embargo on Cuba,[28] which is still in place to this day, thanks mostly to the lobbying pressure of many of the right-wing Cuban-Americans who currently reside in South Florida—those same Cuban-Americans who benefit from this embargo, and in whose best interest it is to continue to see their former countrymen suffer from an antiquated economic blockade.

I have also interviewed a number of these Cuban-Americans as well, many of whom are quick to criticize the Cuban government for its "broken" system. Many of these people left the country shortly after the revolution because they knew that the nationalization of the United States' businesses in Cuba was imminent. They were the ones who were benefiting from many of these capitalist endeavors in Cuba. So naturally, they have a lot of resentment toward Cuba. Still, I have to admit that I completely understand that type of resentment, as their comfortable way of life was brought to an end by the revolution.

It could also be argued that one of the main reasons that these individuals still continue to fervently support *el bloqueo* is that they know that it keeps their businesses in the U.S. alive and flourishing. For the record, most Cuban-Americans are allowed to go back to Cuba. Thus, they take full advantage of that privilege by importing things such as clothes and other products that they buy inexpensively in the United States and sell for a profit back in Cuba. Similarly, others take advantage of being able to bring back boxes of Cuban cigars, which they sell back in the U.S. for a high premium. Because of the mystique that surrounds the Cuban cigar, they are coveted by many Americans who want the chance to smoke this "forbidden fruit." In many cases, the revenue they earn from selling these cigars more than pays for their whole trip to Cuba. Naturally, if the embargo were to cease to exist, then their businesses would suffer tremendously, as everyone would have access to these goods and services, not just the lucky few. So clearly for these individuals, it is not in their best interest to see the embargo lifted. In other words, these opportunists exploit the embargo, even at the expense of their family members back in Cuba.

Consequently, a large majority, if not all, of these Cuban-Americans hate Fidel Castro with a passion. In fact, some of Fidel's own family members, including his daughter, Alina Fernández, live in the United States or Europe and continue to criticize the Cuban socialist system. It is notable, however, that many of the Cuban exiles, although they hate Fidel for one reason or another, still like Che Guevara and Camilo Cienfuegos. However, a good number of those exiles also have an extremely strong hatred toward Che Guevara as well. Much of the time, these expatriated Cubans refer to him as an assassin. And that may, in fact, be true, as Che Guevara was allegedly responsible for executing many people during and after the revolution. Be that as it may, I follow their response with the following question, assuming that Che was responsible for mass executions: "Who is more of an assassin, Che for actually pulling the trigger himself and executing countless prisoners of war, or someone like President Truman who didn't personally drop the atomic bombs over Hiroshima and Nagasaki, but ordered the bombing itself ?" I just leave it at that for them to think about.

In fact, when I asked my female friend in Santa Clara that very question, she gave me the following response: "We have an expression here in Cuba that says, 'The one who holds the cow's hoofs is just as guilty as the one who shoots it in the head.'" So according to her analogy, I would say that President Truman is just as much of an assassin as the pilots who followed orders to fly their planes over Nagasaki and Hiroshima to nuke, and therefore, assassinate, countless Japanese civilians. As we now know, many of the innocent bystanders who were fortunate enough to survive the bombings still continue to suffer from the aftereffects of those blasts.

After eating lunch and hanging out with my restaurant friends, I headed out toward the main plaza just to sit back and relax and look around. Just as I was leaving, so was the owner of the *paladar*. Since it was raining, he grabbed a table umbrella from one of the tables—he didn't have a normal-sized umbrella—and came out and walked toward the park with me. It was during that five-minute walk that he really started to tell me exactly how he felt about the current political system in Cuba. It wasn't that he spoke badly about the system; rather, he began to talk to me about both Che Guevara and Camilo Cienfuegos, who were two influential figures in the Cuban Revolution, both of whom were tragically killed shortly after the revolution. Camilo's plane exploded in midflight and "disappeared" on October 28, 1959, only 10 months after the triumph of the revolution. I put disappeared in quotation marks because that was the sign my restaurant friend made with his hands as he told me the story. I had heard this story multiple times, so I just nodded my head as we continued on our way. Many Cubans are very suspicious about Camilo's death because they presume that there was foul play involved on the part of the Cuban government. However, there is no empirical evidence to substantiate that assertion. Additionally, Che Guevara was killed on October 9, 1967 in Bolivia, by Bolivian soldiers who were trained and equipped by U.S. Green Beret and CIA operatives. There has also been speculation regarding the Cuban government's involvement in his death as well. Even at this point, it remains merely speculation.

Then he started to tell to me about something that I had already talked about before coming to Cuba, which is that Cuba is not a full-fledged communist, or Marxist, country; rather, it is what I have begun to call *Fidelismo*, or Fidelism. Cuba, according to what I had known and now, what I had seen, doesn't exactly align with the theories and ideas of Marx, and therefore, is not truly a Marxist or communist system. Communism is essentially putting the theories of Karl Marx (Marxism) into practice. Let me add that Cuba is certainly not a capitalist country by any means. Interestingly enough, the term *capitalism* is sort of a negative term in Cuba, much like the use of the words *Marxism*, *socialism*, and *communism* carry negative connotations in the United States. Leaving aside any value judgments, Cuba is not a pure Marxist society under Fidel Castro. Just to offer a small example to qualify this claim: Marx was staunchly against authoritarianism. Technically, he was against the ruling class, or bourgeoisie. However, the irony is that many leaders who claim to be Marxist ultimately create a system that is autocratic, or authoritarian, in nature—thus ensuring that they remain in power, through repressive measures if necessary, for as long as they so desire. This would seem a bit anti-Marxist, wouldn't it? In fact, it would appear to have more in common with George Orwell's book *Animal Farm* than Karl Marx and Friedrich Engles' book *The Communist Manifesto*.

To support this assertion, my restaurant friend actually used the term *Fidelismo*, unaware of the fact that I had previously used that term in the United States to describe the system that was in place in Cuba. He then said that once Fidel and his brother pass away, Cuba, as a nation, is not going to know what to do because it has been following Fidel and his ideologies for over fifty years. Many Americans would disagree, and therefore proclaim that as soon as they both pass away, the USA is going to "rush in like heroes" and "help Cuba." Both assertions remain untested, since Fidel and Raúl still remain in control of Cuba.

While I was in Santa Clara, I had the opportunity to visit Che's monument, mausoleum, and the museum that tracks his life from boyhood through his death in Bolivia. I have to admit that this was the most emotional part of my trip thus far, because this was one of the main reasons I had to make this trip. I wanted to see the country that Che helped to liberate from Batista in 1959. As I approached the monument, I was overwhelmed with emotion. I didn't know whether I should be sad, happy, or just to shout. Che has been a figure who has intrigued me for years, and to have the opportunity to go to Cuba to learn about the revolution firsthand, and then, to see where Che was finally laid to rest, was something that can only be compared with having the opportunity to go with my friends, Ariel and Zack, to watch Boca Juniors play—and win—in the finals of La Copa Libertadores (2007) and La Copa Sudamericana (2005). These three moments, among others, have a special place in my heart.

Boca Juniors is my favorite soccer team, so to be able to go and watch them play in one of the biggest finals in Latin America, and to win, is something that very few *Bosteros* (Boca fans) get the opportunity to do. It is a once-in-a-lifetime opportunity. And I got to do it twice. As far as visiting the Che memorial in Santa Clara, that marks a different level of importance in my life, because Che was someone whom I have been reading about and studying for years. I even teach a course about him, as a Latin American icon, at my university. So to be face-to-face with one of the most powerful icons of twentieth century Latin

America was, for me, an overwhelming experience. The museum itself tracks Che's life from birth to death; however, something that I found particularly interesting was seeing pictures that I had never seen before of Che's travels through Latin America. There was one picture that really caught my attention. It was a picture of Che climbing Popocatepetl in Mexico City. Based on what I had read about his travels, it seemed like Che Guevara and I shared a similar *mochilero* (backpacker), or better yet, anthrotourist spirit, a spirit that has inspired me to explore new countries and new lands, and at the same time, get to know the people of these places. That is precisely the heart of anthrotourism. And that is why Che found his way into the anthrotourist-worthy quotes in my book *Anthrotourist: An Improvised Journey Through Latin America*.

Concerning Che's remains in Santa Clara, they were put there because he won a very decisive battle in Santa Clara against Batista's troops on December 31, 1958. This would prove to be the last offensive for Batista and his men, as this victory in Santa Clara was what ultimately led to the triumph of the Cuban Revolution on January 1, 1959. This was surely not how Batista envisioned the outcome of his last offensive, as he sent his best men to take on Che Guevara and his guerrilla forces. Unfortunately for them, Che found out that they were coming by train. And before Batista's men had a chance to do anything, Che had used a bulldozer to uproot the railroad tracks and remove some of the spikes that held the tracks down. This strategic maneuver caused the train to derail as it passed by, leaving Batista's men in a state of shock and disarray, and with only one option—to surrender. The train was packed with some of Batista's best soldiers and was full of weapons as well. In addition, the walls of the train were filled with sand that would slow down any incoming bullets and would act as a makeshift bulletproof vest for the men who were planning to ambush Che's men through cutouts made at the top of the wall of the train. This train was appropriated called *El Tren Blindado*, or "Bulletproof Train." Yet, unfortunately for Batista's men, that didn't work out as planned, and his men were forced to surrender.

This battle was one of the most decisive battles in the Cuban Revolution, as it was the final catalyst that gave the revolution the momentum it needed in order to march into Havana and assume control of Cuba. Shortly before the march began, Batista managed to hop on a plane and take a short flight to the Dominican Republic, where he was safe from Fidel's insurgent army. Soon after that, he used some of the money that he had embezzled from Cuba to buy a piece of property on an island in Portugal (Madeira Island) and lived happily ever after.[29]

Given that this battle marked one of the most important victories of the revolution, and that it was Che and his men who were instrumental in this victory, Fidel Castro decided that it was only fair to put Che's remains and the monument in Santa Clara to remind everyone of the importance of this historical moment for the revolution.

After walking from my *casa* to the monument, which was approximately one mile away, and after visiting, via bike taxi, the site of the infamous *Tren Blindado* victory, I had my bike chauffeur drop me off at a place called *La Veguita*. I had read that this place had great coffee, and I wanted to see if they would be able to make me a good *café americano,* which they proved to be more than capable of doing. I was grateful for that because after that emotional visit, I was really in the mood for a good coffee. What *La Veguita* is known for, aside from the coffee that they serve in the back of the store, are the varieties of Cuban cigars that they sell. They have a factory just across the street where they make the cigars. And had I arrived a bit earlier, I would have been able to get a tour of the factory. However, I arrived a bit late, which was fine by me, because at that moment, all I was really interested in was… a good coffee.

There were three ladies in there working, and given that it was not busy at all (I was the only customer), I struck up a conversation about the history of Cuba. As luck would have it, one of the employees had studied Latin American literature. So we sat for about an hour and talked about some of the great writers of Latin America. Of course when talking about Latin American literature, you can't leave out *el Apostle,* José Martí, who is one of the most prolific writers and thinkers of nineteenth-century Latin America, if not of all time. The funny thing was that she knew so much about Latin American literature that I was not only a bit intimidated, but I was hesitant even to tell her that I was a professor of Latin American culture. Nevertheless, once I spilled the beans about being a professor, I admitted that I would love to have the opportunity to teach at *La Universidad de Habana* and be one of the few *gringos* who have taught there during the Castro administration.

After talking with my friends in the tobacco and coffee shop, I decided to go home and eat. All that talking had made me hungry. However, before I left, I had them pick out a really nice cigar so that I could take it back to my *casa* for José as a gift for his hospitality and for his willingness to talk to me about his experiences in the revolution, the Bay of Pigs invasion, and just about everything in between. After buying José's cigar, I set out for *El Parque Vidal* because I knew how to get home from there. But after walking for about fifteen minutes without recognizing anything, I realized I was lost. So I waited for a taxi to come by, hailed it, and had him take me to my *casa*. I told José later that evening that I didn't get a taxi because I was scared of being lost, but rather because I was too hungry to keep walking. He thought that was pretty funny. And he was extremely grateful for the cigar, which he said was good quality. The funny thing about the dynamic between José and me is that he never called me by my first name. Rather, he called me by my middle name, Roy, which was fine by me because I like my middle name. Besides, I was named after my paternal grandfather, who was a great man. However, I am not used to being called Roy, so instead of hurting his feelings and correcting him, I just went with it. I found it was kind of fun to be called by a different name for a couple of days. I made a little sarcastic joke to myself that it made me a bit more invisible to anyone who may have been tracking me.

CAMAGUEY'S HISTORICAL FIGURES AND LABYRINTH STREETS

Of all the good-byes thus far in my travels across Cuba, this was one of the most emotional. José and Inés—even though they only hosted me for three short days and two nights—built a strong bond with me. This was particularly true of José. José reminded me so much of my grandfather, so it was as if I were talking with someone I had known my whole life. His stories were so interesting, and I got the feeling that he doesn't get to share his stories with many people, much less with crazy *gringos* who stop by Santa Clara to see Che's monument. As I was leaving, he gave me a hug and even told me that he loved me. Now, for a seventy-plus-year-old militia man and revolutionary to tell another man *"Te quiero"* ("Love ya"), that is significant.

So it was a sincerely sad good-bye as José told me that he wished that I could stay at least another month at their house. Honestly, I wished I could have too, because not only are they remarkable people, but the rent is cheap and the food is delicious. Just before I jumped in the taxi to head out, he pointed to the sky and said, *"Nos vemos ahí"* ("See you in heaven"). I hardly ever get sad when traveling because you meet so many people on the road that you get used to bonding with them for a few days and then never seeing them again. It's just part of traveling. Yet, this particular good-bye was exceptional, and I will remember it as one of the most memorable episodes I had on this trip, if not in all of my travels in Latin America. My interaction with José and Inés, along with the mystique of Santa Clara's history and Che's monument, made it the most poignant place I had visited thus far in my travels across Cuba.

And so off I went to Camaguey, which was the next leg of my journey across Cuba. During this four-and-a-half-hour bus ride, I had a chance to recognize that Cuba's countryside is one of the most beautiful landscapes I have seen in all of my travels across Latin America. The combination of beautiful royal palm trees set against backdrops of streams, open land with cattle, and beautiful mountains struck me as extraordinarily beautiful. I know that sounds strange because that description can apply to most of the tropics; however, for some reason, I found Cuba's countryside to be extremely breathtaking. Perhaps it was the abundance of royal palms that covered the Cuban countryside, which seemed to accentuate the already-beautiful landscape. I knew that it wasn't that this particular bus ride from Santa Clara to Camaguey was any more lovely than my trips on the western side of Cuba; rather, it just hit me during this particular bus ride how stunningly beautiful the countryside of Cuba really is.

The other thing that I noticed on this trip was all of the socialist propaganda on billboards. This is not the only place I saw these signs and quotes reminding everyone of the purpose of the revolution. I am not entirely sure which style of billboard I prefer: the provocative sexual innuendoes of the capitalist marketing in the United States and other westernized countries, or the overtly socialist propaganda, revolutionary rhetoric, and quotes that occupy just about every Cuban street corner. It is an interesting observation, as Cuba, being founded on Marxist ideals and principles, is free of capitalism, by and large. Thus, there is no need for capitalist advertisements because everything is run by *el Estado*. Conversely, the United States is an economically capitalist country, and therefore, the success of a business is at least partially predicated on its ability to advertise. And naturally, since sex sells, that tends to be the motif of choice among marketing professionals. Still, both systems have a need to advertise.

Although the "in your face" socialist propaganda and rhetoric was a bit overdone, it was surprisingly motivating. It also serves the purpose of offering its citizens a sense of solidarity. On the other hand, the billboards in the United States just make the viewer want to spend money. Their goal is to convince consumers that buying the product that they are advertising will make them cool. And that is what we all want in life, to be cool—something else the billboards work hard at convincing the consumer to believe. After hours of considering these things and staring out at the Cuban countryside, I was glad when we finally arrived in Camaguey.

One of my reasons for coming to Camaguey was to see the mazelike streets that surround the historic district of Camaguey. While I expected something a bit more spectacular than I actually found, I still enjoyed walking through the streets of Camaguey. The reason behind designing a city to be like a maze was to be able to defend it from pirate invasions. Typically, with regard to Spanish-style colonial cities, they tend to be laid out very logically and in blocks, making it easy for people to navigate the city. The problem that began to arise for Camaguey was that these logical city layouts made it easy for pirates to invade and strategically take over and loot the city efficiently. Thus, the mazelike streets made it more difficult for the invaders, helped the city residents defend themselves against attacks, and allowed them to preserve their city and their livelihood during colonial times.

One of the highlights of Camaguey, aside from visiting Nicolás Guillén's place of residence, was most definitely *Café Ciudad*. In fact, this coffee shop in the main plaza of the historical district of Camaguey won my vote for best *café americanos* in Cuba for two reasons: its price of fifty cents per cup of coffee, and its quality. It was probably the best *café americano* that I tasted in Cuba. I ended up spending a number of hours in the main plaza of the historical district of Camaguey drinking coffee outside the *café*, reading, and watching people walk around.

After getting my fill of coffee, I took to the streets to visit some of the historical sites of Camaguey, like the home of the prolific Cuban writer, Nicolás Guillén. Nicolás Guillén was an Afro-Cuban poet, journalist, political activist, and writer who was active during the twentieth century. His poetry is similar to Pablo Neruda's (the Chilean poet and contemporary of Guillén) in the way he used images of nature, and most specifically, the ocean.

Guillén has a poem in his house, which has been converted into a museum, that reminded me a lot of Neruda's poem *"La Ola"* ("The Wave"). For me, it has been interesting to visit the homes and haunts of many of the writers and historical figures that I studied throughout graduate school. It was as though I could finally put a face to a name by visiting their country of birth and the home where they spent most of their lives. Of course, Che was an exception because he was born and raised in Argentina, yet his commitment and devotion to the Cuban Revolution and subsequent government reforms are the qualities that make him such a prominent figure and icon in Cuba, as well as other parts of the world, such as Bolivia.

Another interesting historical figure that lived in Camaguey was Ignacio Agramonte, one of the major figures who fought in the War of Independence against Spain at the end of the nineteenth century. Cuba was the last Spanish colony to gain independence from Spain. And it wasn't until 1898 that Cuba finally gained its independence. That was only a few years after José Martí had died fighting in the war. José Martí, although he was a writer and an intellectual, chose to fight in the war, and as a result of that decision, was killed in battle on May 19, 1895, approximately three years before Cuba earned its independence from Spain. José Martí was Agramonte's contemporary; however, a salient difference between them was that Agramonte was a bit more prepared as a military man and managed to see the war through to the end. Now his house and the giant statue of him in the main square—which is named after him—stand as a reminder of what he did, not only for the city of Camaguey, but for all of Cuba. Agramonte's house is easily found in the center of the historical district in Camaguey, where it serves as a museum in which you can read about his life, and walk through the rooms of the house where he and his family lived.

As I was leaving the house and was about to go down the stairs and back out into the street, I was stopped by two women who worked at the museum and who asked where I was from. After I told them that I was from the United States, one lady asked me if I would be willing to take her friend back to the United States with me to marry her and make her a U.S. citizen. I laughed this off, as it was a strange and awkward situation. When I told them that I didn't think that "my girlfriend" (I really didn't have a girlfriend, but that was the best reply I could come up with on the spot) would approve of my bringing home a Cuban wife, they suggested that I find an old rich man for both of them. I told them that they would have to compete with all of the gold-digging women in the United States, and if they don't speak English, then that may make it tough to compete in such a tight market. Apparently, they didn't care, and continued talking about how they would work hard if only I would find them two older men around seventy years old. Eventually, I decided it was time to end this conversation, and I told them that I would take pictures of them, and once I found some older men for them, I would send them to Cuba to find them at the Agramonte house. Finally, after taking pictures with the two women, I was able to leave and resume walking around Camaguey.

A noteworthy thing about Camaguey was that of all of the cities I visited across Cuba, it had the most beggars. Until I got to Camaguey, I didn't seem to have any issues with people begging for money. However, Camaguey had its fair share of beggars. And they were clever, too. I am not usually the type of person to give panhandlers money, because although I want to help people, I feel that simply giving them money does nothing more than perpetuate the idea that begging for things is acceptable. Nonetheless, it was hard for me to say no to one of the elderly ladies who was asking me for money. Furthermore, it was kind of tough to act as though I didn't have any money, because I had a small stack of coins (one dollar's worth) on the table that I was going to use to pay for two coffees. However, when the elderly woman approached me and asked for my spare change, and then pointed to the money that I had sitting on the table, I couldn't resist. Although I said no at first, as she was walking away, I thought, *She could be my grandmother.* So I called her back over and gave her the money. And even though she could have been doing that all day, and could have accumulated fifteen to twenty dollars' worth of money from naive tourists, I felt good for helping her. That is a bit ironic, honestly, since I don't generally condone that type of behavior, either on the part of the beggar, nor on the part of the giver. But, hey, there is always an exception to the rule.

On my last full day in Camaguey, I met an extremely interesting girl by the name of Annie who was from Oregon and who was about to start working on her PhD in public health in the upcoming fall semester. I struck up a conversation with her after eating lunch at a *tapas* (Spanish appetizers) place near the main square of Camaguey. She was sitting there with her *Lonely Planet* book on the table, so it was obvious that she was a tourist. After talking to her a bit about what she was doing in Cuba, I was in the mood for a coffee at *Café Ciudad.* Assuming that she liked coffee (as reasonable people do), I invited her to join me. It was pretty cool to meet Annie. She was an extremely fun person to talk to, and she was intelligent, which made it that much more interesting to talk to her. We ended up walking around Camaguey and talking about all sorts of topics, from Cuba's socialist system to her topics of interest for her upcoming PhD program. I was intrigued by her research interests because it was related to things I had not yet thought much about. She was interested in noninfectious diseases in the developing world, which are developed-world diseases that people get in the developing world. Examples are different forms of cancer, diabetes, and so on, which tend to be diseases found in developed countries and regions such as the United States, Western Europe, Australia, etc. It was fun to walk around and talk with her about her academic interests. In a weird way, I felt like a tour guide, even though it was only my second day in Camaguey. And it was nice to walk around with someone for a day, because when you travel alone, it's a nice change to hang out with other fellow travelers from time to time. You might say that it breaks up the conversations that one tends to have with oneself when traveling alone.

For the most part, I enjoy traveling by myself. It gives me a chance to learn more about myself as I travel to new places and am on the road for long periods of time alone. It helps me to become more independent, and it gives me the opportunity to discover myself and to ask myself the hard questions about who I am and what I want in life—questions that many people are scared to confront on a personal level. However, it is in these moments that one can truly discover who he or she is.

The following morning, I said good-bye to Camaguey and hopped on my Viazul bus bound for Holguín. Once I was on the bus, I happened to sit beside a Canadian guy by the name of Chris. He was going to Las Tunas to get a $1 haircut and to visit some friends. He was actually staying in Camaguey and was just going to Las Tunas for the day. Las Tunas is a place that is generally skipped by the average tourist leaving Camaguey *en route* to either Holguín, Bayamo, or Santiago de

Cuba. However, my new friend Chris was looking forward to visiting Las Tunas to get his $1 haircut and to buy some Cuban cigars for his friends back in Canada.

While we were riding to Las Tunas, we struck up an interesting conversation about his perspective on foreign investment in Latin America. After a long conversation about Cuba and Central America, and just as he was grabbing his belongings to get off the bus, I figured it would be appropriate to give him my last copy of *Anthrotourist*. I had given the other copy to Juliet and Andy in Havana because I figured they would appreciate it, especially since Juliet was a professor at the University of Havana and enjoys travel literature. Chris was happy to get the book as well, as I had been talking to him about property options for foreigners in Costa Rica and Nicaragua. Perhaps the book will provide him with some insight into some of the things—both political and economic—that are going on in that region of the world. After I said good-bye to him and gave him the book, the bus left Las Tunas, and we headed for Holguín.

On the way, I drifted off to sleep. Thankfully, I woke up about two minutes before we stopped in Holguín because I would have missed my stop and ended up who knew where. I got up just in time to follow some of the people to the front of the bus to see if I had made it to my destination—this was the first time that Viazul did not stop at an official bus station. Lucky for me, my host was there to greet me. He was calling out my name as I approached the bus door. And even though I was half asleep, I was still awake enough to recognize my name and to get off the bus. However, I almost forgot my luggage, which was sitting in the luggage compartment under the bus. Thankfully for me, I came to my senses in time, and went around to the other side of the bus and got my luggage from the bus driver.

TRIP ONE COMES TO AN END IN HOLGUÍN

After arriving in Holguín and getting settled in my extremely comfortable new room, I decided to grab my *Lonely Planet: Cuba* guidebook and set out to see Holguín. Holguín is also known by most Cubans as "The City of the Parks," because of all the plazas and parks that call Holguín their home. As it turned out, my *casa* was pretty much right in the middle of town, only a handful of blocks away from one of the main plazas, *Parque Calixto Garcia.* That made it easy to get to know the city, as most of the local *Holguineros,* or residents of Holguín, tend to come out in the afternoon and evening to walk around these plazas and parks. As I passed by one of the smaller plazas on the way to *Parque Calixto Garcia,* a group of young kids were playing soccer with something that only seemed to resemble a soccer ball. Nevertheless, they were having a blast. So I stopped for a few minutes to watch them play.

Most of them were barefoot and shirtless as they played with their small, makeshift soccer ball. It was pretty exciting to sit and watch them play and cheer as they scored a goal, as enthusiastically as though they were playing in the World Cup. That is the beauty of soccer, which is in fact called "the beautiful game," by many soccer players and fans across the world. To play "the beautiful game," all you need is something round, a couple of makeshift goals, and a small plot of land on which to play. And there you have it: a soccer game, filled with all of the love and passion that you would find in most official soccer games anywhere. Ironically, Cuba is more of a baseball country than a soccer country. But according to what I have been told, soccer is growing tremendously there.

Take these kids, for example. They used their sandals as goals and an old ball to play with, and they are playing barefoot. The amount of equipment that is required for playing soccer is minimal. That is why soccer is considered the sport of the poor. Baseball requires a bit more equipment, but is still relatively simple to set up and play. I saw kids in the streets using old pipes or even sticks as a bat, whatever they could find as a ball, and their shoes as bases. And so it goes. Sometimes they are so engrossed in their game that they don't even realize that people are trying to get past them on the sidewalk. So as you make your way through the game, you have to be careful you don't get hit with a pitch or a pop fly.

Eventually, after watching the kids play soccer for a while in one of the smaller, adjacent parks, I finally made it to the main park. I had my guidebook with me, and it mentioned a coffee place nearby called *La Cubita*. And since I was in the mood for some good coffee, I thought I would go and check it out. I was a bit confused when I first walked in, because all I saw were a bunch of old Cuban men sitting at a bar and taking shots of *café cubano*. So I walked up to the bar, thinking that it was more or less a coffee bar, and asked for a *café americano*. I was not in the mood to drink *café cubano*. I am not personally a fan of adding sugar to my coffee. When I'm in the mood for coffee – and when am I not – I am not thinking about a shot of sugar. Nevertheless, after I asked for a *café americano* and was laughed at for asking for anything other than the only thing they had on the menu, they poured me a *café cubano* shot and said, "There you go." Apparently, they didn't know what a *café americano* was. However, I didn't complain, as I grabbed my shot of sugar-infused *café*, slammed it down and then asked for another one. After all, beggars can't be choosers, can they?

After a couple of shots of coffee (and at least a pound of sugar), I set out to see if there was anything going on that night that was of interest to me. This time, I was not interested in *La Casa de la Música* or *La Casa de la Trova*, which had been staples for me in other cities. However, given that they had a large, beautiful theater in the park, I thought that I would see if there was a performance that night. I walked across the park to find that there was in fact a play that was about to start. But to my dismay, there were no more tickets. So instead of getting to see a Cuban play, I just went back home to relax and hang out with my family. I also needed to talk to them about other fun and interesting things to do for my last couple of days in Holguín—and, sadly, in Cuba. After chatting with them for a while, we worked out a plan to get me a ride the next morning to a fishing village called Gibara, which was about forty minutes outside of Holguín. They recommended that I do a day trip there because the town is small and it would be better to go, spend the day, and then come back to Holguín in the evening.

The next morning, I met up with my taxi driver, Marcos, and he took me to Gibara. Marcos, who is twenty-one, has two jobs: he is a schoolteacher at the local high school during the school year, and a taxi driver on weekends and when he is on vacation from school. He has to work two jobs because being a teacher in Cuba only pays him about $20 a month, whereas working as a taxi driver pays him a bit more, at least in theory. A taxi driver like Marcos, who does not work for the State, pays about $30–$50 per month to the government in taxes and fees. Anything that he makes above and beyond that is his. However, gas is expensive, and on top of that, his car is thirty years old, a 1983 Lada from Russia. It was actually made in the days when Russia was the Soviet Union, which means that the car parts are not cheap. Despite all this, by working as a taxi driver, he is able to make some extra money so that he can take care of his mother, his younger sister, and his girlfriend, who is currently studying to be a curator in order to work for a museum. Needless to say, there isn't really any money left over for himself after helping with all of those expenses. So I was happy to pay Marcos the $25 that he was charging me to drive me to Gibara, show me around, and then drive me back to Holguín.

Gibara happened to be in the middle of their Carnival, which meant that there was lots of music, lots of people selling things, and plenty of drunken locals. According to what Marcos told me, a pint of Crystal (one of the national beers of Cuba) cost about thirty-five cents. The interesting thing to note is that even though thirty-five cents seems cheap to us in the United States, it is not at all cheap for the average local fishermen from Gibara, who probably make approximately $15 a month if they work for the State. If that is the case, then if they were to drink five pints of beer at thirty-five cents per pint, they would have spent almost one-fourth of their monthly salary on beer. When you look at it from that perspective, it would be like the average American, who makes approximately $2,500 a month, going out and buying pints of beer for $150 each. That would make you think twice before overindulging, especially since that money also has to be used for buying food and other necessities for getting you through the month. Not to mention that the subsequent hangover is not what one would consider a good return on investment. Nevertheless, that didn't keep them from overindulging in lots of heavy drinking, at least during Carnival.

Marcos and I walked around the town, took a few pictures of the scenery, and finally checked out Gibara's. I had originally thought that I would be going to swim, given that Gibara is on the north Caribbean coast of Cuba; however, there were really very few places to swim. So we just strolled around the town looking for a place to eat lunch. We ended up going to a place that appeared to be a combination of a *paladar* and a *casa particular*. We had gotten pretty hungry, so we asked if they had food, and since they did, we decided to eat there. The fact that the food was cheap made it that much more attractive.

I went in and sat down in what I thought was the dining area; however, apparently that was just the front of the house, as our hostess/waitress/cook escorted us through what seemed like a secret labyrinth until we got to a small outdoor area that had a couple of tables underneath a thatched-roofed, tent-like structure. It came as a nice surprise, except for the handful of flies that were buzzing around. Overall, the place was nice, and since eating outdoors in the Caribbean and having flies hanging out with you go hand in hand, they were no more than a minor annoyance. You just have to know how to protect your food and drink by putting napkins or something on top of it to keep the flies from landing there. Our lunch was amazingly large and tasty: a huge plate of shrimp in a red sauce, tons of rice and beans, and a delicious, freshly-cut spread of vegetables, all for $10. I decided that I would treat Marcos for taking the time to show me around. Also, I knew that even though it was only $5 per person, that would have been a large chunk of his monthly salary as a schoolteacher. So I was happy to treat him so he didn't have to worry about it.

After a great lunch and a trip to Gibara, Marcos told me that he would take me to see *La Loma de la Cruz* (the Hill of the Cross), which was back in Holguín. Originally, I was going to walk to *La Loma,* which stands at the top of approximately 456 stairs, on the top of the mountain that loomed about ten blocks from my *casa particular.* But since Marcos offered to drive me there, I took him up on it. It is no doubt great exercise for anyone who wants to do some extreme stair-climbing in the hot Cuban sun, and I had actually been looking forward to making the trek because I felt that taking a taxi to the top was a bit of a cop-out. Nevertheless, since we were already on the road and on our way back to Holguín, and since Marcos told me that he would just drive me up to the top so that I could check it out and take some pictures, I took him up on the offer, and we drove to the top of the *loma,* or hill, to check out the cross.

The cross was put at the top of the hill in 1790 because the town had been suffering from a major drought, and they believed that if they were to put a cross there, then it would be pleasing to God, who would therefore send rain. I never found out whether or not that actually happened. Still, it must have brought some sort of blessing, as the cross is still there. It was replaced with a larger cross years later. Additionally, in the mid-1900s, they built a staircase to the top of the hill, the construction of which took twenty years. And now it makes for an "easy" 450-plus step climb to the top. The cross is still used as a place where people bring offerings and prayers, particularly in May, when the people of Holguín celebrate *Romerías de Mayo* ("the May Pilgrimages"). On May 3 of every year, numerous *Holguineros* make the trek to the top of the hill to take part in a large Mass service at the cross.

After I had walked around and learned a bit about the significance of the cross, as well as stared down these 456 stairs out into the city—and realized how long the walk would have been from my *casa particular*—Marcos took me to the main plaza near my *casa* so that I could walk around a bit more and take some pictures. I was really fortunate to have met Marcos. He was an excellent tour guide, and in addition, we had a lot in common. We spent a lot of time talking about the difference in the educational systems of the United States and Cuba, which, interestingly enough, are very similar in a lot of ways. For example, the Cuban school schedule is on the same schedule as the

U.S., maybe due to the historical influence of the U.S. Another extremely interesting example is that the students say a "pledge of allegiance" in grade school just as they do in the U.S.; however, instead of pledging to "...the United States of America," the Cuban pledge contains the statement, "...*pioneros por el comunismo. Seremos como El Che*" ("...pioneers of communism. We will be like El Che").

One of the main differences, however, aside from higher education being free in Cuba, is that to earn a bachelor's degree, a student needs to take five years of school, as opposed to the United States' system, where it takes the average student only four years to complete the required 120 credits (fifteen credits per semester for four years). I had to explain to Marcos what a credit was since they do not use the same terminology with regard to college classes.

We also had plenty of time while we were driving around and walking all day to talk about his perspective on the political system of Cuba. Marcos seemed to be very supportive of the revolution, even though he complained a bit about the salary that he received working for the State. He also acknowledged that the economy of the State was in no condition to give all State employees—approximately 85 percent of Cubans living and working there—a pay raise. And for that reason, Marcos had to work as a taxi driver in his spare time to supplement his income to help his family.

Regarding his overall opinion on the current administration, Marcos said that he would estimate that only about 10 percent of the population would consider themselves strongly opposed to the Castro government—ironically, estimating the exact inverse of what the woman in Santa Clara had thought.

A good example of a group of people who are staunchly against the Castro administration are *Las Damas de Blanco* (the Women in White). These women march in Havana as a form of nonviolent protest against the Castro administration. Some Cubans have said that they are funded by a U.S. agency or organization. However, there is no empirical evidence to substantiate that claim. While the Cuban government claims this organization of women is being funded by the United States, it is noteworthy that these women appear to be free to speak their minds publicly. In fact, I was told that the Cuban police and other members of the local government infrastructure such as the CDR

(*Comités de Defensa de la Revolución,* or loosely translated as "Committees for the Defense of the Revolution") send people out to protect these women from locals who try to throw rocks and projectiles at them in an attempt to put an end to the nonviolent protests.

Reading about it in the U.S. media, it is not framed this way; the U.S. media describes the CDR as imposing a direct violation on these women's human rights. But the people who are violating their human rights are not the police, Marcos said, but rather local residents who are trying to put an end to the seemingly peaceful protests. The police and other local agencies are dispatched in order to keep the peace. I have not personally been a part of these events, so I cannot confirm or deny this; this is simply what I have been told by local residents who spoke to me about these women "objectively."

Nevertheless, this group of women overtly despises the Castro administration. What I find interesting is that they are not arrested and thrown into jail as a result of speaking out against the government. While I have heard varying opinions and perspectives on the level of freedom of speech that Cuban citizens have, this is one of the few concrete examples I was able to look at.

Some people told me that there was an extremely high level of police-state-like repression imposed on Cuban citizens that limits their freedom of speech. I was told by one Cuban that people believe that there are cameras in the streetlights, and that they are used to spy on people. However, that would be extremely costly and would require a relatively high level of technology, a cost that the Cuban government is, more than likely, unwilling to add to the budget. Furthermore, that would be a bit extreme, even for the most oppressive dictatorships (e.g., Argentina from 1979-1983 and Chile in the 1970s and 1980s under Augusto Pinochet). And those dictatorships were, in part, supported by the United States as part of Operation Condor.

On the other hand, I have also spoken with Cuban citizens who tell me that they are free to openly express their discontentment with the government and its policies; still, it wouldn't be a good idea to go out into the street and scream, "I hate Castro!" That would be, first and foremost, deemed as disrespectful, and secondly, as being subversive. I see it as a bit ignorant too, because even though there is a small percentage of disgruntled Cubans who are openly dissatisfied with the way

Cuba is being run, one could make the argument that Fidel has, at a minimum, set up a system that provides those very same people with health care, free education, and a small monthly ration of food. Whether or not those three things are provided in a sufficient way is an entirely different argument—what can't be argued is that the Castro government at least tried to provide these things to everyone.

Nevertheless, whether or not people are free to speak their mind, screaming at the top of your lungs that you hate the president is definitely playing with fire in any country. I was told that Cubans are free to express their unhappiness towards a specific policy or issue pertaining to the Cuban system; however, simply saying that you hate everything would not be taken seriously and could put that person in jeopardy of being denounced, or reported to the local CDR. The CDR is an organization established to monitor the local community. Each set of blocks has its set of CDR members that oversee the neighborhood like local vigilantes. They have a registry of everyone who lives in the community, their occupation, and so on, and they are meant to be a grassroots-level service that looks after the safety of the community. This was how it was presented to me.

In stark contrast to this altruistic description of the CDR, some skeptics said that the CDR was established to monitor what could be considered any subversive actions against the government. They compared the CDR to a local-level big brother system. This is cheaper and more efficient than putting cameras in the streetlights, as some people feared.

A local CDR office is set up as a committee with a president, vice president, and other officers, and is also responsible for having meetings where people can (theoretically) openly discuss different issues or disagreements they have pertaining to the local government. Those issues are then moved up the bureaucratic ladder to the higher-ups in the government to determine whether or not the complaint is legitimate and worthy of changing or making a new policy that would make the community, city, or country better, thus perpetuating the revolution's ideology.

This structure allows members of the community to share ideas and discuss policies with the CDR and local government agencies. As I have already mentioned, any attempt to call out or denounce the government in its entirety, or the president specifically, is not tolerated. Interestingly enough, the case of the *Damas de Blanco* remains an anomaly, as I was told that the CDR had, on occasion, protected these women from acts of violence against them. In the case of these women, the CDR actually ends up serving as a sort of riot police, protecting the protesters from the rest of the community's residents.

Hearing such different perspectives showed me clearly that the seemingly repressive measures of Cuba's "big brother" is, perhaps, not as black and white as the media suggests. Naturally, the anti-Cuba propaganda machines in the United States want to make people believe that it is an extremely oppressive regime that rounds up, imprisons, and executes any person that says anything at all against the government. If that is the case at all, it is certainly not as prevalent as the U.S. media alleges. That's not to say that historically (circa. 1959–1991), the administration has been free from that type of repression. But before being too quick to judge Cuba, let's not forget that the United States has been convicted of repressive behavior and foul play as well. In fact, the International Court of Justice (ICJ) in the Hague, Netherlands, ruled in favor of Nicaragua in 1986 in a case brought against the USA for violating the sovereignty of Nicaragua by aiding the Contras, as well as mining Nicaraguan harbors during the Nicaraguan Civil War.

Another troubling point was, if you even suggest that Fidel Castro was in any way, shape, or form responsible for the deaths of Camilo Cienfuegos (his plane exploded in midflight, and no remains could be found) or Che Guevara (captured and killed in Bolivia), you risk getting up to thirty years of jail time. That was a topic that Cubans did not publicly mention, even though many of them shared their opinion with me in private. One cannot ignore the fact that what the United States would consider freedom of speech, meaning the ability to openly criticize or speculate about the government or the president, is essentially nonexistent here in Cuba. However, few Cubans would consider themselves oppressed and miserable. On the contrary, numerous Cubans told me that they feel extremely free in many ways. They pointed out that they don't have the stress of worrying about paying for rent, health care, education, and food. All of this is provided by the government, whether you work or not. Even those who choose not to work are still guaranteed food, affordable housing, free health care, and free education. Moreover, the choice to contribute to the Cuban society is up to each individual. If you choose to live outside of that society and not contribute to it, you fail to help sustain the Cuban ideology and revolution. Nevertheless, the government still respects you as a human being and gives you the minimal implements for survival.

One of the shortcomings of this system, in terms of financial compensation, is that the difference between someone who chooses not to work, and a doctor who has fifteen years of education, is minimal. One of the original—and primary—objectives of the Cuban Revolution was to create a more egalitarian system in Cuba, as well as to raise the standard of education nationwide by making it accessible to everyone. Unfortunately, those who are educated and play a major role in the society (e.g. doctors, nurses, teachers, etc.) are not compensated accordingly by the State. This can be attributed to lack of funds, which otherwise would be allocated to these individuals' salary. However, much of the government's resources are being allocated to those who choose not to contribute to the society at large, thus abusing the system and draining it of its resources. That, in my opinion, is one of the major flaws of the current system. Furthermore, that was one of the inherent flaws in Che's idea of the *new man* as well.

Assuming that a society as a whole is going to work for one another altruistically, simply because they are interested in the society's success as a whole, has historically proven to be an unsustainable system. This is not to say that the whole ideology is flawed; rather, failing to incentivize the ambitious citizens of a society can lead to both a domestic and international brain drain. This is not the same as advocating for a deregulated, free market system either. I am just suggesting that failing to provide adequate incentives for the hardworking Cuban citizens will inevitably lead to the collapse of the socialist society as a whole, because it fails to compensate those that work hard and contribute to the success of the society, while having to spend resources supporting those who choose not to work. In other words, if there is no difference, financially speaking, between those who work hard and those who consciously choose not to work, then the system will fail to economically sustain itself. The problem with Che's ideology was that he assumed that everyone was as hardworking and/or as altruistic as he was. And unfortunately for him, and Cuba as a whole, that is not the case. In short, something needs to be done at a governmental level to provide incentives to those that are contributing to the larger society, and to penalize those who choose to do nothing. History has shown us that a social system cannot rely solely on altruism. So the question still remains: How do you guarantee all of your citizens all of the basic needs with which to live, but at the same time, motivate people to be the best that they can be so that the society as a whole can progress?

Additionally, the issue of tourism must be addressed in order to keep other members of society from leaving the traditional Cuban structure and joining the peripheral society, which is comprised of businesses catering to tourists. That society is stealing members from the mainstream of Cuba simply because it pays better. And although it is still part of Cuba, the members who work in this arena are not necessarily contributing to the overall well-being of the revolutionary government. This is what I refer to as a domestic brain drain, as opposed to an international brain drain, which is where the educated people of a given society leave their country of birth to live and work in another country because the economy is better and they can make more money elsewhere.

After spending the day talking about economics, public policy, and tourism, among other topics, Marcos, his girlfriend, and I decided to spend the evening drinking coffee (because obviously I needed more coffee by now). And since we had pretty much exhausted just about every social and political topic we could talk about, we just hung out and talked about my overall experience in Cuba. I told them that on the whole, I really liked Cuba. Yet, with regard to its system and ideologies, it would be something that I would have to meditate on for a while, because it was an extremely complex system that was in complete ideological opposition to the one in which I had grown up.

Something that I found to be a bit funny (and a bit of a relief) was that Marcos and his girlfriend had no clue what Facebook was. I think that they were the first two people that I had ever met in the world who had not heard of Facebook. In fact, most of the Cubans that I met had no idea what Facebook was, because most Cubans don't have access to the Internet. At $6 an hour, it is a bit expensive for the average Cuban, even if they were permitted to use these cafés, which they are not. Instead of making any conjectures as to the reasons behind why Cubans aren't allowed to freely surf the Internet, I chose to just explain what Facebook was, and that many Americans waste countless hours on Facebook when they could be doing more productive things. But, hey, who am I to judge how they spend their time? They are Americans, and they live in the "Land of the Free," right? I have found, after a visit to Cuba, that "freedom" has many more definitions than I had thought. Americans are free in the sense of political expression and the right to own a weapon; however, free in terms of health care and education? ...Not so much.

After drinking a couple mediocre *café americanos* (they were really a simulation created by combining too much espresso and some water), we decided to walk home. After all, we needed to get a good night's sleep since we were going to spend the next day traveling around the northern coast of Holguín.

The next morning, we made our way to Banes and Guardalavaca (which interestingly enough, does translate to "Guard the Cow") to tour an archeological site called *Chorro de Maita* in Banes, and then go check out the beach at Guardalavaca. The site at *Chorro de Maita* was discovered as people began to develop the area and build houses. One day, as someone was digging a foundation for his house, he discovered that he was digging into an indigenous cemetery (I guess the bones gave it away). So before digging any farther, he called in the professionals, archaeologists and anthropologists, to see how old these bones were. It turned out that the site was a Taino Indian burial ground, which was part of a Taino community. As a way to preserve the site, they erected a museum around it so that visitors could see the skeletons as they were buried over five hundred years ago.

This is not to say, however, that the Spanish marched in and slaughtered these indigenous people, as they so often did in the New World. According to the site itself, and the layout of the bodies, it seemed apparent that in this case there was actually a peaceful coexistence between these indigenous people and the Europeans. Of course no one alive now was there, so scientists can only speculate. Nevertheless, one of the bodies that was buried there, according to the archaeologists who have studied this site, was assumed to be a

European who cohabitated with this particular group of Tainos. This was determined by comparing the skulls of the indigenous people who were buried there with the odd skull that was also buried there alongside the other members of the community. The European skull had different characteristics from the Taino skulls, and furthermore, it resembled the skulls of other Europeans—specifically Spaniards—that were historically found in the Americas as well. On further study, it was determined that all of the members buried there appeared to have died from natural causes. In fact, the position of the bodies led the experts to ascertain that these individuals were all buried ritualistically and were not dumped into a mass grave site. This includes the European who was buried there. Many of their bodies were adorned with gifts and memorabilia.

Even though it has been assumed that these indigenous people died of natural causes, there is some evidence that at least one of the members was possibly strangled to death (or hanged) as a way to avoid having to do slave labor, which was assigned to them by the Spanish conquistadors. So even though there was not necessarily any bloodshed as there might have been in battle, there was evidence to show that some of the members of this society successfully committed suicide in order to avoid being subjected to forced labor. Apparently, that was their only way to avoid becoming slaves. During the Conquest and subsequent African slave trade (15-18th century), the Spanish were merciless, as they were trying to extract as much gold and other valuables from the indigenous people as possible. Once they had successfully worked the indigenous people to death, quite literally, they began to bring African slaves over to continue where the indigenous people left off, in order to perpetuate the Spanish empire in the New World.

It wasn't until 1898 that Cuba and its people were able to free themselves from Spain, thanks to José Martí and other liberators such as Máximo Gómez and Ignacio Agramonte. And then, around 1959, another revolutionary by the name of Fidel Castro took over and was able to liberate the Cuban people once again. This time it was from the imperialist power to the north, the United States of America. And whether or not "history will absolve him,"[30] we have yet to see, as those pages are still being written.

After checking out this beautifully preserved site at *Chorro de Maita*, Marcos, two of his other friends, and I went to Guardalavaca to hang out, swim, and just relax on my last full day in Cuba. I couldn't have asked for a better last day. Guardalavaca is a little bit on the touristy side, but given that it was the low season in Cuba, it was not crowded at all. In fact, the beach was relatively empty, which was great for us. The beach of Guardalavaca is in the northern part of Holguín Province and stretches as far as the eye can see with turquoise water, beautiful white sand, palm trees, and sea grape trees. While I was enjoying the beach, I had a chance to sit and talk with one of Marcos's close friends, Ana. The two of them grew up together, studied the same subject—physical education—and taught at the same high school. Marcos was studying to get his master's degree. Then he plans to get his doctorate, a feat that, here in Cuba, won't cost him a penny, except for some extraneous living costs.

Marcos's friend, Ana, was a beautiful and intelligent Cuban girl who loved her country, even though she was not a hundred percent in agreement with all of the government's policies. But then again, who is a hundred percent in agreement with any government? Perhaps people who have not taken the time to critically analyze their own political system would be a hundred percent in agreement, but to any thinking person, that kind of blind agreement is impossible. In fact, I would go so far as to say that no political system in the world, thus far, has proven to be perfect. Ana told me that if she had the opportunity to go visit other countries, then she would love to do that. However, she would not stay, as she loved Cuba and was grateful for what her government offered her in terms of health care, education, and her overall quality of life. As a qualifier, she did argue that the health care system was not without problems. She put a lot of blame on the nurses. She stated that, although they were highly trained, they weren't paid well ($30–$40 a month salary). And as a result, they weren't very hard-working.

Even though she was happy living in Cuba, she was well aware of the flaws within her government, as she had a brother who moved to Europe and had been able to send her information about her own country that is "hidden" (as she put it) from the citizens. Nevertheless, she was still content, and took full advantage of the opportunity to get a free education. In addition to going to school and teaching physical education at the local high school, she took care of her grandmother, who had cancer. At the end of the day, we had to rush home after the beach because she needed to get back to help with some medical procedures.

So, after a great day at the beach, we got back, I said my good-byes, ate dinner, and started to pack, as I had to return to the United States the following morning.

FAREWELL TO BEAUTIFUL CUBA

There are those occasions when you don't want to leave somewhere. Typically, it is when you connect with a place so much that it seems like a part of you is being left behind. Those occasions are few and far between; yet, when you make that connection, it makes it that much harder to leave a place. That was how I felt in Cuba. And saying goodbye to Marcos, Ana, and everyone else that I had met in Holguín was tough. In fact, each place that I visited, and each person that I met along the way, had really left a mark on me in one way or another. Cuba deeply affected me, and I felt that it was going to take some time to digest all that I had experienced, from the politics to the beauty of the country itself.

After getting dropped off at the airport, I again assumed that I would run into some trouble with Customs, given that I was an American citizen; however, it seemed that the process for Cubans going back to the United States was much more onerous, as they had to provide Customs with considerably more information than was asked of a regular tourist. Not that I was a "regular" tourist, given the embargo the United States maintains against Cuba. Ironically, it was the opposite when I got back to the States. It appeared that the Cubans were questioned much less than I was. Even so, being stopped by the U.S. Border Patrol was still a very easy experience. They were extremely friendly and gave me little to no problems, especially once I showed them my affidavit allowing me to do academic research in Cuba. All in all, the process seemed to be a breeze. Ironically, the hardest part of the whole process was finding a ride home from the airport, as my friend (who will remain anonymous) forgot that I was arriving, and wasn't around to get me. Thankfully, my roommate and his girlfriend came to the rescue.

After traveling across Cuba and getting a better understanding of their system and seeing their way of life firsthand, I found myself a bit meditative and in need of some reflection. I had grown up in the United States my whole life, apart from living for short periods of time in other countries in Latin America, and had become accustomed to living in an extremely capitalist system, a system that caters to the intrinsic human drive to do better. Now I had been given the opportunity to see a country whose economic and governmental systems are the exact opposite of the United States. In fact, it is a system that is arguably in a class of its own, as it is one of the last true socialist systems of its kind remaining. I cannot say that Cuba's system is a failure, because I saw many things about their system that, at least superficially, seemed to work well.

When talking about Cuba, I am referring to a country that is considered to be developing, and therefore, as I have discussed, would be better compared to countries such as Haiti, the Dominican Republic, and Honduras, who, among others that I have mentioned, are also considered developing nations. And despite the fact that it is a developing country with no natural resources, they have been able to seemingly guarantee all 12,000,000 citizens food by means of the "Canasta Básica Alimentaria (CBA)," which, even though it's supposed to last a month, generally is only sufficient for two weeks; free education for all who are capable of passing the necessary exams for moving forward in a particular career and who can handle the rigor of the program; free health care with access to doctors, surgeons, and most medicines, limited only by their availability (and, ironically, sometimes the cost of those medicines in CUCs); a house for which Cubans pay little to no rent; and low electric bills. Of course, I shouldn't romanticize this, as there are some important caveats for this particular set of rights as they are provided to its citizens. For example, although school is free, the burden of taking care of students while they are attending school becomes the responsibility of the parents, who have to save even more and cut back their spending in order to budget for their son's or daughter's school expenses. It could be argued that this is no different from most families in the United States who save up and budget in order to help their son or daughter with college bills. The difference is that tuition in itself is free. It is only the living expenses such as food and clothes that the parents have to subsidize in order to allow their son or daughter the opportunity to study and become whatever it is that he or she is studying to be. Naturally, this is a significant sacrifice on the part of the parents; however, the relatively low cost of living allows this to be possible in most families across the country. This is certainly something that distinguishes Cuba from many of its colleague nations in the developing world: the opportunity to go to a university and study to be what one dreams of being, insomuch as one can meet the academic requirements.

Knowing all this, I am confused at why the American propaganda machine continues to tell people that Cuba is such a bad place. I am not suggesting that the United States should adopt Cuba's ideology. On the other hand, I am also not suggesting that Cuba adopt the United States' ideology either. One must assess which ideology works best in a particular country. Certainly Cuba's system would not work in the United States; however, one could also argue that the extremely capitalist model in the U.S. would not work in a place like Cuba. To get a better sense of what that would look like, all you would have to do is look at how Cuba was in the early 1950s under Fulgencio Batista's corrupt, U.S.-backed, authoritarian government. Moreover, we could use other countries such as the Dominican Republic, Honduras, and Guatemala as a litmus test for what Cuba could possibly be like if the United States were to implement their neoliberal economic ideology in Cuba. In most of these countries, statistics have shown that over the last thirty years, the rich have increasingly become richer and the poor have increasingly become poorer.

Clearly, the neoliberal policies that were implemented in these countries have not been good policies with regard to stimulating local infrastructure, economic growth, and upward mobility, as these countries have statistically failed to reduce the gap between the rich and poor. That was essentially what the neoliberal policies proposed by the Washington Consensus sought to do in the developing world. Of course it looked great on paper (much like Marxist theory); however, when put into practice, it raises a whole plethora of questions. In short, what looks good on paper may not necessarily work well in practice. And in my opinion, that is what we are seeing in much of Central America: a failed system. That is not to say that the same system would have failed everywhere; but it appears to have not worked in much of the developing world, and more specifically, Central America.

After this trip, the question continued to nag at me: why was I taught that Cuba was bad?

Is Cuba "bad" because their ideology is different from ours? Is Cuba "bad" because they will not allow the United States to impose their hegemonic ideology on them? Is Cuba "bad" because they sided with the Soviet Union during the Cold War? Is Cuba "bad" because they strongly oppose the U.S. government's foreign policy?

I cannot find a legitimate reason why we should still be *angry* at Cuba. I understand that Fidel nationalized all of the foreign businesses in Cuba without recompense shortly after the Cuban Revolution, so I concur with the original justification for the embargo. Nevertheless, at this late date, one could make a strong argument that the embargo is being abused and exploited by the Cuban-Americans who seek personal financial gain, and therefore use the embargo to their advantage now that they are here in the U.S. On the other hand, one could also make the rebuttal argument that the embargo, on the side of the Cuban government, is being exploited and used as a way to justify the lack of progress in Cuba, thus keeping the Cuban people in a state of perpetual shortage. It could therefore be said that the embargo is simply a pawn in the game of political chess between the U.S. and Cuba.

Our dislike of Cuba is certainly not because Cuba has a dictator in power, but rather because that dictator strongly disagrees with our foreign policies and agendas. We not only like and support, but have also trained dictators such as Somoza, Pinochet, and Noriega, just to name a few. We have had no problem with dictators if they obey the United States and adhere to U.S. demands and restrictions. After going to Cuba and observing their way of life, I made every effort to try to objectively understand how their way of life could be considered such a threat to the United States. I understand that having sided with the Soviet Union during the Cold War, and particularly during the Cuban Missile Crisis, definitely put Cuba on the "bad" list in terms of bilateral relations with the United States. But if one recalls that prior to the Cuban Missile Crisis, the U.S. had nukes in Turkey aimed at the USSR, it would only make sense for the Soviet Union to retaliate and use Cuba to strategically place missiles ninety miles off the coast of the United States. It's hard to blame them for doing that, assuming that the United States had their hand on the button too. It's important to acknowledge the level of fear that *both* Russians and Americans were subject to as a result of this crisis.

Still, taking all of that into consideration, and taking into account the sanctions and embargo placed on Cuba after all of this transpired, I am wondering why the U.S. media still demonizes Cuba, when, in all reality, this tiny island nation cannot possibly be a threat to U.S. national security. I think much of the hatred has been created by the media. Of course I cannot leave out the fact that Castro's administration has its propaganda machines too. I am just asking myself, *Why?*

In short, I feel like I have walked away from this trip even more baffled than when I left. There are so many interesting questions that I may never have answers to, both on the side of the United States, as well as on the side of Cuba. Perhaps one day the United States and Cuba will reconcile their differences, or then again, perhaps we will have to wait for another generation to pass away so that the younger generation, who are not as emotionally attached to the situation and history, can start afresh and repair this broken relationship.

INTERMISSION
BETWEEN TRIP ONE
AND TRIP TWO

There was a one-month interlude between the first trip to Cuba and the second trip to Cuba. During that time, I had the opportunity to return to Virginia and North Carolina to spend time with my family. I was even coerced by my brother to go skydiving with him for his thirty-second birthday. This was the first time in my life where I had the sensation of *traveling*; however, in mid-flight, I was forced to jump out of a perfectly good airplane. Moreover, while I am used to flying, and thoroughly enjoy it, opening the airplane door at fifteen thousand feet to jump out was certainly a unique experience. And even though this defied all logic, it was an exhilarating experience that I got to share with my brother on his birthday.

After skydiving and spending time with my family back in the USA, I headed back down to Latin America; this trip took me to the beautiful Caribbean island of Roatan, Honduras, where I met up with some of the members of the nonprofit sport and development organization, CAN Fútbol Foundation, Inc. (CANFF). I spent one month working with their on-the-ground directors and resident intern on development projects in and around Oakridge, Roatan, which is a community on the eastern end of the island. It happens to be a community that is at-risk, socioeconomically speaking, as it has a bad reputation for drug trafficking and prostitution, among other things. It was precisely for that reason that CANFF decided to implement their first-ever program in Oakridge in 2008. By combining their love for soccer with their passion to make a difference in their own community, CANFF could mobilize large groups of people to carry out grassroots-level development projects. All of this was to be spearheaded by their director in Honduras, Luis Alvarado, who, over the course of the last five years, has begun to transform the community with the help of the young soccer players who live there. For more information about what CANFF is doing in Honduras and other parts of the world, visit their website at www.canff.org.

After working in Honduras for one month, I had the opportunity to go back to Cuba and finish my tour of the country. My first trip was from Pinar del Río in the west to Holguín, which is toward the eastern part of Cuba; however, it is not part of *El Oriente*, which was a place that I wanted to see on my first trip, but had to forego because of time constraints and funding. Fortunately for me, I was able to go back to Cuba a second time, and finish traveling around the eastern part of the island to explore some of the most unique parts of Cuba—most notably, Baracoa, a place that many people had told me about during my first trip. So it was a must-see for me during my second trip. Another motivation to return was to visit some of the friends that I had met in Holguín on my first trip, as well as to explore other places in the east such as Guantanamo, Santiago de Cuba, and Bayamo. Thanks to some extra funds from my university, I was able to afford a trip back to Cuba to pick up where I left off.

I would like to invite you to join me on the second part of this trip around Cuba, to see how my mentality and perspective begins to change as I found myself integrating more and more into the Cuban society.

GOING BACK TO CUBA

TAMPA TO HOLGUÍN

"Are you an American?" That was the infamous question that I was asked as I stood in line to get my boarding pass for Cuba. That I am among the small percentage of Americans who are permitted to board a direct fight from the USA to Cuba still boggled the minds of even the Cuban-Americans who are flying back to Cuba to visit friends and family. Some had not been back for more than twelve to fifteen years, so for them this experience was similar to that of any other American traveling to a country in the developing world. It became quite entertaining, as I got to see Cuban-Americans (who act more like Americans than Cubans) standing in line and trying to deal with the lack of organization typical of Latin American travel. As for me, I am used to it, and quite frankly, I embrace it, as it reminds me that I am one step closer to being in a region of the world that makes me genuinely happy.

The check-in for this chartered flight to Cuba was even a bit more disorganized than usual, as I had to go to three different stations: one to get a boarding pass, the next to check-in luggage, and the third to pay for the checked luggage. And with the Cuban-Americans taking extra duffel bags full of gifts back home, this lengthy process can undoubtedly test one's patience. So for the traveler who is not accustomed to this type of protocol, it can be a bit nerve-racking and frustrating trying to make sure you are in the right line at the right time and have checked in properly.

The best part about standing in these unorganized lines was being entertained by some of the Cuban-Americans as they prepared to go back to their homeland to visit family and, more than likely, go hang out at *Playa Varadero* (or as I call it, the Cuban Cancun). In fact, with regard to this particular trip, I couldn't help but notice that there were a handful of Cubans wearing shirts with the American flag proudly screen-printed on the front. I found that to be a bit uncalled-for. It is not that I was judging anyone for the style of clothes they were wearing—God only knows that I have probably worn my fair share of bad styles. But I was disturbed by the fact that they would choose to wear a shirt with the American flag emblazoned on the front to Cuba, of all places, especially since they are Cuban themselves. I could only imagine the Cuban Customs officer's face when these people showed up with their Cuban passport and their big American flag T-shirt on. I found it to be a bit confrontational, that's all.

The other amusing thing I saw while standing in line were all the Mr. T. lookalikes waiting to check in their luggage. These Mr. T. lookalikes, as I thought of them, are Cuban-Americans who are decked out from head to toe in gold. I was not sure if it was theirs or if they rented it for the trip just so they could show up to Cuba "blinging" for their family and friends to give the impression that they hit it big in the United States. This sounds absurd, but I was told by numerous Cubans and Cuban-Americans that these Mr. T. lookalikes really do rent the jewelry for their trip to Cuba. If that is the case, then that is even more crude—and pathetic—than the Cubans sporting the American flag T-shirts.

Even before I boarded the plane from Tampa to Cuba, I was informed by one of the flight attendants that Cuba was currently experiencing an outbreak of cholera in the eastern part of the country. There were cases reported countrywide as well. There had even been cases reported in Havana. The interesting part about this was to read the U.S. reports on this compared with the Cuban reports. The Cuban government tried to downplay the number of cases, whereas U.S. newspapers like the *Miami Herald* did quite the opposite. So, as the saying goes, "There's your story, my story, and the truth."

Unfortunately, this cholera epidemic forced me to deviate from the route I had originally planned for this trip. The majority of the cholera cases were in Manzanillo and Bayamo, which was where I was planning to go after leaving Holguín. Bayamo is only a couple of hours from Holguín and was one of the stops I had planned on the way to Santiago de Cuba. Bayamo is famous for its chess fanatics. It is a normal occurrence to see people in the parks and in designated areas of town playing chess. So I was hoping to go there to play and attempt to redeem myself after losing at chess in Havana. Apparently, the Cubans know how to play chess exceptionally well. And for good reason: they were taught by the Russians, who are known for their world-class chess players. But in order to avoid running the risk of contracting cholera, I tentatively took Bayamo off my list of destinations, at least until the cholera outbreak had subsided.

Once I arrived in Holguín, I visited with friends that I met on my last trip, in May and June of 2012, and caught up with them. Actually, I knew what they had been up to because we had been e-mailing, so it felt more like a homecoming. The first night that I was there, I stayed out until midnight with my friend Ana playing dominoes in the street with her and her neighbors. She and I were a team, and were total amateurs. Still, by some miracle, we managed to beat the people we were playing, who actually knew how to play dominoes and were really good at it. After winning the game, which was actually a series of games, I told them that I was officially retiring from the game of dominoes so that I could go out as a winner. Then I taught them about the saying "beginner's luck," or *suerte de principiante,* in Spanish.

Throughout the forty-five minutes that we were playing, though, I was a bit on edge. We were playing dominoes quite literally in the street while cars from the 1950s, Chevrolets, Fords, and old Russian Ladas, drove past us in the narrow streets of Holguín. I could easily imagine one of them not paying attention and plowing right into us. I couldn't quite understand why we weren't sitting on the perfectly good sidewalk that was beside us. Apparently, this was what they did every night, and according to them, no one had ever been hit that they could recall. Come to think of it, it was probably safer doing this there than in the United States, since no one in Holguín was texting and driving as people so commonly do in the United States. These drivers actually had their eyes on the road. But never mind the danger, it was a fabulous experience being out there with the neighbors, playing dominoes and assimilating into the community as though I had lived there my whole life. It didn't take long for them to start joking about how bad I was at dominoes; however, I guess you could say that Ana and I had the last laugh, as we ended up winning.

It was really interesting how such a small gesture, like playing chess or dominoes, gave me access into their world. If I had not been leaving the next morning, I would have stayed out all night playing dominoes. I was planning to go with Ana and her friends to Levisa, which is a town about sixty miles to the east of Holguín. In fact, it turned out that we needed to be at the bus terminal at 6:00 a.m., which meant that we needed to start walking to the terminal at 5:30. So I had to wake up about 4:45 a.m. in order to have time to eat breakfast (and have coffee) before starting out.

This adventure would be new and interesting because it involved riding on a local Cuban bus line (Astro Bus), which was not an entirely legitimate thing for tourists to do, per se. Astro Bus Line, as a local bus line, is significantly less expensive than the tourist bus line, Viazul. Technically, you need a Cuban ID to get a bus ticket on Astro, which prevents any non-Cuban resident from getting a ticket. Typically, the tourists are directed to a bus line like Viazul that only goes to the major cities across the country, whereas this was a local bus, so it not only goes to the major cities, it also stops in the smaller towns out in the countryside. I had to use my friend's brother's ID, which I could do because he wasn't traveling with us. I did not do anything that was technically illegal; rather, I just did something that most tourists don't get to do, which was to ride a local bus that took me far from the tourist areas. I was so far away from the areas meant for tourists that there were neither hotels nor *casa particulars* in the area, which obliged me to do another thing that most tourists do not have an opportunity to do, which was to stay in a real Cuban home and get a true taste of rural Cuban life. If I were to have done that in a city such as Holguín, Havana, or Santa Clara, then the family where I stayed would have run the risk of being denounced for hosting a tourist without being an approved *casa particular*. In this particular case, those rules didn't apply, because I was so far away from any hotel or *casa particular*, that I couldn't stay in one even if I wanted to.

Staying with my friend's family in Levisa was unforgettable. It was a true bonding experience, as we were a total of eleven people in a two-bedroom, one-bathroom apartment. For anyone who has a problem living with people they barely know in close quarters, or sleeping on a mattress pad on the floor, this would have been unbearable. But for me, it was fine. The only thing that freaked me out a bit was the presence of the large tarantulas that lurked outside at night. They never made it into the house, though, as we killed them before they got close. When it was bedtime, we shut the door so tight that they couldn't get into the house in the wee hours of the night to crawl onto any of us.

The other thing that was a bit surprising was the fact that José, one of our friends, decided to turn the music on full blast at 8:00 a.m. And even though *I* thought that was a bit strange, no one else seemed to complain at all. Apparently, it was quite normal to blast Cuban reggaeton that early in the morning. In fact, it's likely that if José hadn't done it, then one of the neighbors would have. And if they had, it would probably have been the same music: reggaeton, salsa, and a hodgepodge of music in English. More than anything, I was entertained listening to my Cuban friends trying to sing the words to Adele's song "Set Fire to the Rain" without really understanding a word. Apparently Katy Perry, Adele, and Pitbull were more popular here than I would have thought. I hadn't heard one Pitbull song played on my trip from Havana to Holguín, and I was pleasantly surprised to hear it now. It seemed that even the Cubans had been infected with music from Pitbull.

The bus trip to Levisa was exciting because I was not technically supposed to ride on the local buses. So I had to keep my mouth shut and not talk until we had boarded the bus and left the station, because we didn't want to run the risk of them kicking me off for not being Cuban. Because of my physical appearance and familiarity with the culture, I can pass for a Cuban when I keep my mouth shut. Thankfully, everything worked out well, and we headed for Levisa without any problems. I found that the buses were about the same as Viazul buses in terms of the quality of the vehicle itself. The only difference was that the tourist buses had a bathroom, whereas on this bus, there were seats where the bathroom would be. So we just had to hold it if we needed to go to the bathroom. And keeping that in mind, I didn't drink too much coffee for breakfast that morning.

The bus took the same route through Holguín that the Buena Vista Social Club sang about in their famous song *"Chan Chan,"* which made me feel, in a surreal way, that I was in the song: *"De Alto Cedro voy para Marcané. Llego a Cueto y voy para Mayarí."* In English: "From Alto Cedro I go to Marcané. I get to Cueto and then I go to Mayarí."[31] They probably had been going by bus too (or, in Spanish, *guagua*). But finally, the sleepiness of the early morning won the battle between surrealism and sleepiness, so I dozed for a large part of the ride. I couldn't help it; I had gone to bed after midnight, and woken up at 4:30 a.m.

In Levisa, we cooked out and went to a couple of local hangout spots, most notably the local beach, named Corinthians, and a local river. The three main objectives of the trip were to celebrate our friend's birthday, to be with her family who were living in Levisa, and to celebrate the twenty-sixth of July. Levisa was a small rural town outside of Mayarí (not that Mayarí was a large town by any means), and many of the people lived there because they worked at the nickel factory. Apparently, the nickel that was extracted here in Cuba was primarily exported to Canada, much like sugar was exported to the U.S. before the trade embargo. Many of the local people worked in the nearby factory, as it provided them with a stable job. The only downside was that Levisa was out in the middle of nowhere. It was a big change from being in Holguín, which, even though it was not a big city by any stretch of the imagination, was still a formal *city*. In Levisa, we stayed in an apartment building that was only about one mile from the bus terminal. It was so close that we walked to the apartment from the terminal when we arrived.

Many of the residents of the apartment building worked at the factory. The apartments themselves were set back a bit from the road and were next to train tracks, banana plants, and some pigs (who I believe may be owned by the residents, and, I'm certain, will become food in the near future). The apartments, like many buildings here in Cuba, lack aesthetic maintenance but are nonetheless well-built with concrete and rebar. The interior of the apartment boasted a nice-size kitchen, a full bathroom with running water, a living room, and two bedrooms. This, by developing-world standards, was pretty nice, especially as the structural integrity of the building itself was strong. They had ceramic tile floors, and they had a full bathroom complete with a shower with running water and an indoor toilet. Those are luxuries that many people do not have in the developing world. These amenities made hosting eleven of us feasible.

Regarding the twenty-sixth of July, it was the name and date associated with the Cuban Revolution. On July 26 in 1953, the first attempt at a revolution was launched: an attack on the Moncada Barracks in Santiago de Cuba. This event was significant because it was the precursor to the Cuban Revolution, in honor of which the revolution itself adopted not only the arm band, but its name: the twenty-sixth of July or *"Movimiento 26 de Julio"* (M-7-26). It was an exciting experience to be in Cuba on that date because they celebrate it as their independence day. And in a way, it does mark a certain independence, or separation, from the old way of life, which was highly controlled by the United States. It was interesting to see how people decorated their apartment buildings for the occasion. They used recycled plastic bags and hung them on a string or line so that they could hang and sway in the breeze. They also took miniature twenty-sixth-of-July flags and stuck them in bamboo, then stuck that bamboo in a larger piece of bamboo, and finally, they set them on the ground to line the front of the apartment building. To my disappointment, there were no fireworks set off at midnight. Fireworks, it turned out, are not sold in Cuba. Still, there were definitely some victorious-sounding shouts as the clock struck midnight, and of course, lots of loud music and rum. And even though the day itself is undeniably political in nature—much like the 4th of July is in the U.S.—the celebrating, in itself, transcended people's personal political views; beyond any political overtones, it was an opportunity to have a great time with friends and family.

Regarding the idea of "revolution and rum," and contrary to what one may think, the rum company Bacardi was originally from Cuba. Usually, if you were to ask most people where Bacardi is from, they would tell you that it is from Puerto Rico, which would be incorrect. The Bacardi family was in fact from Santiago de Cuba; however, after the revolution, they decided to move their factory and the family to

Puerto Rico in order to avoid having their company nationalized by the new revolutionary government headed by Fidel Castro.

In fact, as the Bacardi family was packing their bags (and their recipe) to make the move to Puerto Rico, they were told by the new Cuban government that they wouldn't be allowed to leave Cuba if they didn't hand over the recipe for Bacardi rum to the Cuban government. Eventually the Bacardi family relinquished the recipe, closed their factories in Cuba, and left the island to start afresh in Puerto Rico. The Barcardi family was able to start up the rum company under the same name, and it has since regained its popularity. In the meantime, the Cuban government, using the old Bacardi recipe, reproduced their own version of Bacardi rum with the new name Havana Club.

The following morning, we all woke up (with more music starting at 8:00 a.m.) determined to do something adventurous, as everyone was tired of being cooped up in a small apartment in the middle of nowhere. At least, I know that I certainly was. However, as I sat on the porch that morning listening to everyone try to make plans for the next day and a half, I couldn't help but overhear them continue to bring up their concern about the cost for a *guagua* to take us to the beach or to the nearby river. It seemed that we weren't ever going to be able to do anything, because it was going to be too expensive.

So after drinking a couple Cuban coffees *sin azúcar* ("without sugar"), I went inside to talk with José and inquire how much it would cost for all of us to go and spend some time at the beach or at the river. After all, we were out in the country, so I guessed that it couldn't be too expensive, but I really had no idea. José told me that for $30 we could rent a *guagua* that was large enough for everyone to ride in. Even the huge pig on the long, wooden skewer, our intended dinner, had room to join us. And for that price, the driver would take us to the beach that day, wait for us, drive us home, and then do the same for us the following day at the river. For me, that sounded pretty inexpensive. On the other hand, for my friends, spending $30 as a group (approximately $3 each) would be like an average middle-class American spending almost $300 dollars per person for the equivalent trip. At those prices, it would make you think long and hard about whether or not the beach or the river was going to be that much fun. To save them the trouble, and to alleviate any hint of stress or anxiety, I told José that I would pay for the whole thing. As I told him, "This is what I save my money for: to be able to enjoy spending time with my friends." I had barely gotten that out of my mouth before José's face lit up with excitement, because he knew how much fun we were all going to have. I had no clue what was in store for us, but I was very willing to invest in the experience.

The beach that we went to was called Corinthians, and it was a beautiful Cuban beach with miles of white sand stretching out into turquoise Caribbean water. And as if being there was not exciting enough, we brought the pig on the skewer along. We had slaughtered and cleaned it that morning so that we could cook it in a fire pit on the beach while we swam. I have to admit that slaughtering a pig for the first time was an eye-opening experience. For anyone who doesn't have the stomach for seeing that, it would have been a gruesome sight. And the sound of the pig screaming as it was being stabbed would have emotionally scarred someone who couldn't handle seeing animals getting killed.

We decided that it would be better to let someone else do the dirty work, since we were going to be at the beach, and didn't want to have blood and pig hair all over us when we got there (I am sure that this imagery alone is enough for most readers). Nevertheless, someone had to do it, and for $2, one of the neighbors killed the pig and then he and his friends cleaned it for us. So after the pig was killed and cleaned, we took it along with the rest of the food we were bringing to the beach. The funny part about the beach outing was that it took the pig so long to cook over the open fire that we didn't even have time to eat the food at the beach before our ride home arrived. By then, the sandflies had started to become bothersome as well. So we had to take the food (the pig on the skewer and all) back to the apartment to eat it there. Nevertheless, it all worked out well, and we had a phenomenally delicious meal.

The head and some of the other pig parts that were left over and not eaten were used the following day to make *caldosa*, or stew. We ate that the next day for lunch at the river. The stew was made with the leftover pig bits, some of the pig fat for flavoring, plantains, and some local Cuban vegetables. All of that was simmered together for hours to give it a delicious flavor. Then, once it cooled, we squeezed fresh lime juice over it, and it was ready to be eaten. It was the perfect meal after a day of swimming in the river.

The river itself was beautiful. The main section where most of the people congregated was a bit crowded, with people jumping off rocks, cooking food, and drinking Cuban rum. This was a place where the local Cubans come to hang out. This simple getaway was all most of them could afford, given that the majority of them work for the State and earn very little. While the food cooked, a few of us took a trail upstream to a place empty of other people, and where the water was a clear jade green. It had just about everything you could want there except for a waterfall—deep spots, small pool-like rock structures, and fresh flowing water, so we spent a couple of hours hanging out there and swimming. It was breathtaking, as we were in the middle of the wilderness, surrounded by mountains and a beautiful river that we had all to ourselves, with refreshing water to swim in. After several hours, we went back to our *palapa* (which was really just a makeshift tent with some towels to sit on and a few chairs), ate an amazing lunch of *la caldosa* before swimming a bit more; and at last we headed back to Levisa to pack up and return to Holguín.

THE *HOLGUINERO* EXPERIENCE

One of the interesting things about the Cuban people and their vibe for life, or as the French would call it, their *joie de vivre*, is that the Cuban people find the smallest ways of entertaining themselves. Presumably, the Cuban people have learned to become resourceful as a result of their lack of material items, due in part to the low salaries as well as the United States-imposed economic blockade. The low salaries limit their amount of disposable income while the economic blockade limits their access to foreign goods and services.

As a result, their entertainment tends to be very modest by U.S. standards. For example, as I was walking back from one of the parks in Holguín, I saw a guy dancing salsa, alone, outside of a window. At first glance, I figured that he was just dancing while he was waiting for someone; however, as I got closer, I realized that he was painting the window sill. He had the music playing from his house, and while he was painting, he was dancing salsa to the music. That gives a whole new meaning to the phrase "whistling while you work." He was in his own world, dancing and painting.

In fact, watching this guy in action made me consider the concept of escapism. And the thought of escapism sparked the idea that traveling could also be considered a form of escapism. Of course, the word in itself means exactly that, to escape from something. At the same time, it doesn't have to imply that you are escaping from anything bad. You could simply be escaping from your normal life and relieving yourself of all the day-to-day responsibilities that life throws at you. So it could be said that traveling provides that type of escape, and could therefore be considered a form of *escapism*. Look at it this way: when you travel, you typically go to a place where you can travel around, learn about new things, and meet new people, or else it is a vacation where you want people to wait on you hand and foot so that you can, as many would put it, "veg out."

No matter which your preference may be, many of us could classify this type of travel, whether it's the all-inclusive resort-style vacation, or a backpacking trip somewhere off the beaten track, as escapism. Either way you look at it, these types of adventures, or vacations, allow you to leave your comfort zone and your daily responsibilities in order to enjoy and be part of something that is new and unique, or just different from your daily routine. The idea of escapism does not require that you leave the country; you just need to get away to a place that allows you to escape your day-to-day routine and lifestyle. It's when you have managed to give yourself the luxury to choose to do *what* you want, *when* you want it, and *how* you want it, that you have experienced the idea of escapism. Many people travel to a faraway land via books, which could also fall under the category of escapism; but in this case, I am referring to the physical form of escapism, which takes the very physical form of traveling.

In my case, I find that traveling allows me to escape from my day-to-day routine. It also allows me to assimilate into other cultures, which is the essence of the idea of anthrotourism: to consciously integrate into the cultural framework of the society in which you are traveling and living. This approach allows you to escape your life back home, and therefore, allows you access into another way of life and another way of thinking. That is one of my primary objectives when I travel: to try and learn about other cultures and people in order to get a deeper glimpse into their way of seeing the world. In other words, it allows me to see the world through their eyes, thereby escaping from my own world, if only for a short time.

While staying in Holguín, I had the opportunity to live in the community and get a real sense of the day-to-day life of the people who lived near my *casa*. Going to Levisa with Ana and her friends allowed me to get to know all of them much better, and as a further benefit, it provided me a group of people with whom I could hang out in

Holguín. And even though I had only known most of them for less than a week, they treated me as if I were family. It was interesting that I was able to bond with them and earn their trust in such a short period of time. Because it wasn't all that difficult, it gave me the insight that the Cuban people in Holguín were extremely friendly and really enjoyed meeting new people and spending time with them.

I was also very impressed with what my friend Ana did for her father for his birthday. She saved up her money for months just to be able to hire a group of *mariachis* to come and sing to him—and the neighborhood—at midnight on the day of his birthday. Just to put things in perspective, to hire a full band of *mariachis* in Cuba costs approximately $120, which, given the average salary of between $20 and $50 a month, would take months to save up for. Nevertheless, this was something that she wanted to do for her father, and it turned out to be a total success. When I asked her why she went to such great lengths to save up and do this, she said, "This $120 is not even a drop in the bucket for all of the money my father has spent to raise me." For her, it was a pleasure and an honor to be able to do something nice for him. That type of sacrifice and gesture for family members is not out of the ordinary in Holguín. And to me, that was what made these people so special. What was even more impressive was that, even though most of them just met me less than a week prior, they still treated me as if I were a lifelong friend, or a neighbor.

It was remarkable to see people who lacked so many material things possess such a *joie de vivre*. Not that material possessions can ever make people happy. Quite the contrary, I believe it leads people down a road of materialism and selfishness that prevents happiness. That selfishness and discontent appeared to be nonexistent for the most part, because the Cuban people, as a result of *el bloqueo*, have been theoretically cut off from the materialistic and capitalistic temptations of the United States. This has, in turn, forced them to learn how to be resourceful, to make things last, and to value non-material things.

I went into my friend's house and was surprised to see the nice refrigerator and microwave that they had in their home. She told me that the only way she was able to afford to buy those appliances was because her husband brought them back from his medical mission in Venezuela. Furthermore, she said that it would have been nearly impossible to buy a refrigerator like the one that she had on a regular salary. She added that they had to fix their house in phases, as the money comes in little by little. The other memorable thing that she added, and her friends concurred, was that the people of Holguín typically pride themselves on fixing up their houses and focus less on other things, such as expensive clothes. Ironically, Holguín's residents still know how to dress for less. Whereas, according to my friend, the people of Havana would prefer to live in a not-so-nice place and have nice clothes, nice phones, and nice *stuff*. That was one of the differences between the people of Holguín and Havana. My friend Alejo added that he would rather walk around in sandals, shorts, and a T-shirt, and have a nice bed to rest his head on at night than "style out" all day with nice clothes, and at the end of the day, sleep on the floor.

Up to this point in my travels, I'd had nothing but wonderful experiences throughout all of the provinces of Cuba in which I had traveled, so naturally I expected things to continue in that vein. Still, it is entertaining to hear the Cuban people compare themselves with one another. Even though Cuba is an island, it is quite large and extremely diverse. Cuba is actually one of the larger islands in the world, spanning approximately 1,200 kilometers in length. This makes for many subcultures within the larger Cuban culture. In fact, my friends joked about the people of Pinar del Río in the same way that people make "blonde jokes" in the United States. Apparently, the people of Pinar del Río were an easy target. Although Pinar del Río was an extremely beautiful place with delightful people, just like anywhere in the world, there is always *that* group of people who are the butt of the jokes. And here in Cuba, that happened to be the people of Pinar del Río.

After being at my friend Ana's house for her dad's birthday, we all decided to go to the park and hang out for a little bit. While I was sitting in the park, I had a chance to talk to Ana about her brother and his situation in Cuba as a university student. Apparently, he was accepted into an extremely competitive program at the university; however, when they were at a symposium, he gave a presentation that highlighted some of the flaws in the Cuban government, which resulted in his expulsion from the university. His presentation was seen as an attack on the current administration, as he exposed certain things that were not, for lack of a better term, public information. This type of penalty for expressing your true feelings in Cuba can be felt and seen among many of the Cuban people. In fact, even though I said in previous chapters that there was a certain freedom of speech in Cuba, I think that it would be suitable to qualify that statement, as many people who choose to express themselves do so while looking over their shoulder or talking quietly among trusted friends.

At the same time, I would argue that Cuba has a lot to offer its people and is surely one of the most beautiful countries that I have ever visited. Nevertheless, for the Cuban people to be truly free, I think that there needs to be a higher level of freedom of expression. I am convinced that for human beings to truly evolve as individuals, they need the freedom to express themselves without the threat of being persecuted or imprisoned for differences of opinion. I am not saying that everyone needs to exercise the right to bash the president; rather, I am suggesting that the freedom to express oneself—be it artistically, politically, or musically—should be a valued and respected freedom in Cuba.

BARACOA AND
EL ORIENTE

The trek from Holguín to Baracoa started early in the morning with a 6:00 a.m. departure, and with Carlos, the owner of my *casa*, and I having to push-start my friend Marcos's 1983 Russian Lada in order to restart it after he had turned it off to wait for me to get my stuff and load the car. From there, we picked up Carmen and her daughter at their house and made our way to the place where we would look for a ride. Her husband followed us on his bike to help out with finding a driver who would take us to Baracoa.

The trip itself was broken into two legs: The first leg was from Holguín to Moa, which was close to Levisa, where I had been with Ana and her friends. In fact, we took the same route that I took to Levisa, which took us through Cueto, Mayarí, Levisa, and eventually, Moa. This was not the traditional tourist route, as the roads were not the best roads that I had seen in my travels across Cuba. Nevertheless, it was a fun ride because I was able to see a part of Cuba that I would not have seen had I taken the tourist bus line, Viazul. This ride was much more comfortable than my return ride from Levisa with Ana and her friends. In order to return from Levisa, we rented a truck that was an old, French school bus that had all of its seats ripped out and replaced with wooden benches. It was far from comfortable. Nonetheless, it was inexpensive, and it was large enough to carry all eleven of us, and the gear that we had brought with us, back home to Holguín, so I didn't complain.

The truck I was in this time was, in fact, pretty comfortable, and to top it off, I was riding "shotgun," right up front next to the driver. The truck itself was like something out of a 1950s mafia movie and was dark purple, which made it easily recognizable as we were driving to Moa. Our driver's friends could see us from hundreds of meters away and they threw us a thumbs-up with a huge smile on their face. The ride from Holguín to Moa was trouble-free, even though the ride itself was almost three hours. The best news was that the roads appeared not to be as bumpy this time—perhaps because I actually had a cushion on my seat as opposed to sitting on a bare wooden bench. So the drive was far less painful than the one from Levisa to Holguín.

I was traveling with Carmen, who was a friend of the owner of my *casa,* and her daughter. Her husband was one of the people who helped us rent the *jeepe* (pronounced jeep-eh) that we rode in. He also helped to negotiate the price for the next part of our journey once we got to Moa, and located another driver to take us from Moa to Baracoa. Apparently, most drivers from Holguín don't like to drive from Moa to Baracoa because the roads are extremely bad. Baracoa used to be virtually cut off from the rest of the country due to poor transportation infrastructure, which was why their cuisine and their vibe made their visitors feel as if they were in another country. That's not to say that the energy in the rest of Cuba was bad; rather, Baracoa had its own cultural identity since the bad roads had kept it segregated from the rest of the country until shortly after the Cuban Revolution. After the revolution, there was a project spearheaded by Fidel Castro and Che Guevara to open up access to Baracoa as part of their initiative to unify all of Cuba.

Having to arrange for another car in Moa to take us to Baracoa was a whole aggravation in itself. Thankfully, I was with someone who had done this before, and who was from Baracoa, and who was willing to take on this headache by himself, saving me much stress. We managed to get a truck that took us to Baracoa for close to the cost we had agreed to in Holguín, give or take a couple dollars. However, I think that our driver was in a bit of a bad mood because he couldn't find one more person to fill the single vacant seat that he had in the back of the *jeepe.* As we drove toward Baracoa, he was looking to add one more client to the trip. Unfortunately for him, the only person that wanted a ride was a guy who only needed to go up the road about ten kilometers.

Instead of paying the $2 it cost to go to Baracoa, he only had to pay about fifty cents, which upset our driver even more. Because now he was full, but not with a passenger that needed to go all the way to Baracoa.

Once we dropped him off, a little farther up the road we stopped where an elderly woman was waiting with her grandson. Apparently the boy had hurt his leg and needed to go to the hospital; however, they had no money. Yet by some human miracle, our driver—even though he was in a bad mood—told her to get in and have her grandson sit on her lap. There was really only space for one more. I asked our driver what was going on, and he looked at me and said, "She is an old lady, and even though she has no money, we have to help her." And without hesitation, I looked back at him and said, "Don't worry, my friend, I will pay for them." He just reached his hand out, and with a big smile, he shook my hand as if I had made his day. I was deeply touched by his generous gesture toward this woman. And being caught up in the moment, I just reacted. In reality, $4 is nothing for most people in the developed world. But, for these people, it meant the world. Besides, there is no better way to kill a bad vibe than by doing a good thing.

Yet with regard to a "bad vibe," I could not forget the vision of the nickel factory that we passed as we were leaving Moa on our way to Baracoa. Apparently, Che Guevara had inaugurated this factory shortly after the Cuban Revolution in 1959 and had worked there as a volunteer; the factory was even named after him. However, this factory looked like something out of *The Simpsons*. As we approached it, aside from seeing the smoke pouring out of the chimney, we saw a sign that said, "Do Not Take Photos." And for good reason: it was a hideous sight. What used to be the landscape that was downwind was barren and looked like something out of the movie *The Terminator* after everything had been burnt and destroyed. The water from the river that flowed away from the factory was the color of antifreeze. It was actually quite a depressing sight to see. (The chocolate factory in Baracoa that Che inaugurated in 1963 made up for the factory that we passed in Moa, as you could smell the aroma of cacao—chocolate—from hundreds of meters away. As we passed the factory, I couldn't help but make a joke by referring to it as "Che and the Chocolate Factory."

However, all kidding aside, the taste of the chocolate was just as good as the smell.)

Finally, after what seemed like forever on the bumpy roads between Moa and Baracoa, we made it to our destination, and were welcomed by beautiful landscapes, rivers, and the Caribbean Sea. It was love at first sight for me. In any case, we were welcomed with all of the beauty of the Caribbean, and it was certainly a sight for sore eyes. Not that I was tired of Holguín, but it was nice to be at the beach again. As we drove through Baracoa, *en route* to our *casa,* I couldn't help but think about how much this city reminded me of the landscape that one would see on the eastern end of Roatan, Honduras, where I worked with the nonprofit fútbol organization, CANFF, and which is one of my favorite places to spend my spare time. My *casa* in Baracoa was the same one where Carmen and her daughter were staying. In fact, it was Carmen's mother's *casa particular.* Carmen had even delayed her trip for a couple days in order to ride with me and make sure that I got there without any problems—a gesture for which I was grateful.

Eventually, after driving through Baracoa for about thirty minutes, we finally made it to downtown Baracoa, which was where the majority of the people lived and where the *jeepe* driver dropped us off. Baracoa is located in the far east of Cuba, in an area known as *El Oriente,* and, as I mentioned, Baracoa was physically separated from the rest of the island for most of its history. Their culture, cuisine, and other Baracoian elements continued to evolve on their own, uninfluenced by the outside world. Thus it became a province that is unique in all senses of the word. As soon as you get to this city, you begin to see and feel the distinctiveness. Of course, things such as music were universal across Cuba, but the food and the way of life in Baracoa were entirely different. Given that Baracoa is a coastal city, it is blessed with seafood and a lifestyle that lends itself to a more relaxed beach atmosphere. Not that anywhere is Cuba really appeared to be tense; however, Baracoa was one of the most relaxed places that I visited on my travels across Cuba.

After setting my things down at my *casa,* I decided to walk around town and try to locate a couple of friends whom I was supposed to meet in Baracoa. My two friends, Katie from England and Maria from Germany, had been in Santiago de Cuba and were traveling around *El*

Oriente at the same time I was. So we all decided that Baracoa would be a perfect place to meet up. It just so happened that we were arriving the same day, which was just a coincidence, since trying to plan things in Cuba was next to impossible. Remember my meeting in Havana with my friend Jessika and her friends? What made it so tough to arrange was that the Internet cost $6 an hour, and in addition, the Internet cafés were a long walk from the *casa*. Also, purchasing a phone was next to impossible for foreigners, as well as quite expensive for everyone, including Cubans. So the fact that we were able to meet up in Baracoa within one day of arriving was little short of miraculous. The fact that Baracoa was a small city did make it easy to find one another. I e-mailed Maria and Katie my address and they came and found me.

After joining up with Katie and Maria, and consulting with Carmen, we decided that we would take a trip to *el Yunque* National Park the following morning to swim in the waterfall there. And if that wasn't enough for one day, we decided that it would be a great idea to finish the day kayaking on the *Río Toa* (or Toa River). *El Yunque* waterfall was part of the river that ran throughout the national park and was overlooked by *el Yunque* itself. *El Yunque* is an approximately 580-meter monolith that seemed to be in the shape of an anvil, if seen from a distance, which was what gave it the name of *el Yunque*, or The Anvil. To hike up to the top of *el Yunque* required a good amount of water and quality hiking shoes, so we decided to hang out at the waterfall and jump off the rocks into the plunge pool of the waterfall instead of making the climb; some of the people who came with us did not have the proper shoes or were not planning to make that sort of hike.

The hike to the waterfall was still about forty-five minutes long, walking uphill, climbing over rocks, and ultimately, arriving at one of nature's beauties, the waterfall. I was a bit disillusioned when I arrived because I imagined the waterfall to be much bigger; nevertheless, it was still breathtaking, and a great place to spend a few hours climbing and jumping off rocks, sitting under the falls, and swimming around.

After hanging out at the waterfall for a few hours, we packed up our belongings and walked to one of the little houses that was along the trail. Unbeknownst to us, the family had made fresh fruit and coffee for us to eat and drink. And after stuffing ourselves with bananas, pineapple, and mangos, we left—though not before asking them, "How much do we owe you?" And the owner of the house said, "Whatever you feel like leaving." So we left them approximately $3, which was one-fifth of what most Cubans make in a month. Apparently, that was a good tip—and well worth the money. It was a win-win situation all around.

From there, we made our way out of the park and over to the Toa River, where we were hoping that we would be able to kayak. I did not know whether or not it was even possible, but to my surprise, they had kayaks. And even better, they were in good condition. So we rented a couple of them and made our way down the beautiful river that cut through Baracoa. I had been struck by its beauty on the way into Baracoa. Now it was pretty interesting to be able to see it from the inside looking out. According to Carmen, *el Río Toa* is one of the deepest rivers in Cuba. This worked to our advantage as we made our way to the shoreline, which had a sudden, deep drop-off, where we were able to climb some of the trees that extended out over the river and jump off without worrying about what was underneath. It was so deep that I couldn't touch the bottom, even after diving down as far as I possibly could.

As we were leaving the government-run campsite and park, one of the workers told us a story of a Bahamian guy who was in trouble in Cuba. He told us that this particular guy was wanted by the Cuban police, though he didn't say what it was for. So he came over here to this campsite and began to rent Jet Skis (now there are no Jet Skis to rent—probably because of this guy) to bury different escape provisions in the sand of the beach at the mouth of the river. And one day, after he had all of his provisions lined up and prepared for departure, he rented one more Jet Ski, collected his gear, and took off, never to be seen again. It is assumed that he went back to the Bahamas, but no one knows for certain.

When the camp guide finished his story, we went back to our *casa* in downtown Baracoa. On the return trip, I asked our driver, whose nickname was *Lindo* (which, means "good-looking" in Spanish), if he could stop at Che's Chocolate Factory so that I could take a picture. And of course, he was delighted to grant me this request, as that factory was the pride and joy of Baracoa. Not to mention the mouth-watering aroma—and the chocolate is good as well!

On our ride home our driver, Lindo, began to tell us about some of the "lies" of Baracoa, as he put it. This was a joke amongst Baracoians vis-à-vis some of the tourist sites in the city. For example, one of the rivers near the center of Baracoa is called *El Río Miel,* or the Honey River. Lindo said that this was one of the "lies" of Baracoa because it was not made of honey. Another "lie" that Lindo explained was that *el Yunque* (the Anvil) was not really an anvil, or even in the shape of an anvil for that matter. The last "lie" of Baracoa that he jokingly told us was that he was called Lindo and, as he confessed, he was not good-looking.

Whether or not those things were true or not, does not change the fact that Baracoa was an extremely beautiful and natural place. And it was not only the natural parts of Baracoa that were interesting, but also the sense of history that exuded from this town. In fact, this city was host to Hatuey, one of the most famous and rebellious *Caciques* (chiefs) in Taino history. Hatuey rebelled against the Spanish conquistadors and was eventually burnt at the stake. However, before he was executed by the Catholic conquistadors, he left the world with a famous story. He was asked by the Catholic priests if he wanted to accept Christ, and therefore, go to heaven, before he was burnt to death. Hatuey asked, "Do Christians go to heaven?" One of the arrogant Catholic men then replied, "All good Christians go to heaven." And Hatuey said to him, "Then send me to hell."

This is an interesting perspective, as Hatuey saw heaven—or the place where the conquistadors go when they die—as a place full of oppression and oppressors. So naturally, if his idea of the Spanish heaven included being subjugated for eternity, then it was only natural that he would want to go to another place. So his conception of hell was a place where he would be away from the Catholics, the conquistadors, the pillaging, and the greed. And who can blame him? Why would anyone want to go to a place where they feel like they are going to be subjugated for all eternity? The heaven that the Tainos envisioned for themselves was certainly not a place of subjugation and oppression.

The Tainos themselves left some beautiful cave burial sites in Baracoa. Most notable, at least to me, was *La Cueva de Paraíso* (or Cave of Paradise), which was a series of cave structures in the hills of Baracoa that served as a burial site for the Taino Indians. In one particular cave, it was believed that some of the remains that were stored there belonged to a Taino *Cacique*. The Tainos didn't live in the caves; they were the place where they chose to bury their dead, because it was seen as a great resting place. They believed it was the place that was most connected to the spirits of the afterlife. An added benefit was that it was protected from the rain and other elements that would erode the earth, and consequently destroy their burial site. So to be able to walk through this archeological site and see the Tainos lying there as they have for hundreds of years was sobering and awe-inspiring. In addition, the view from their burial site was breathtaking, as I could see all of Baracoa from these beautiful caves.

Apparently, *La Cueva de Paraíso* was not particularly unique in Baracoa; on the contrary, Baracoa was sprinkled with caves. In fact, Cuba is known for its caves. Many of them served as places of refuge or burial for the Tainos while they inhabited this part of Cuba. I was able to visit another set of caves by making the five-mile roundtrip walk from my *casa* in Baracoa. These caves are called *La Cueva del Agua,* or The Cave of Water, because there is an underground channel of water running from the ocean through this cave system. Some parts of this cave system were explored by a Russian diver who sought to find an underwater route from *La Cueva del Agua* to the ocean.

As if the cave itself wasn't impressive enough, the walk to the cave was equally amazing. First of all, we had to walk along the beach for approximately one mile, cross a hundred-meter rickety wooden bridge, then walk approximately a mile and a half to the house where the family who found the cave lived.

After the long trek there, when we made it to our guide's home, we were greeted as though we were part of the family. Upon our arrival, they immediately chopped up pineapples and mangos for us. Then they gave us some bananas to eat. And as if that wasn't enough hospitality, they invited us inside their little 250-square-foot house to watch the Olympics on their fifteen-inch TV. We almost delayed our trip to the caves because Cuba was about to compete in an Olympic boxing match, so we all decided that we would gather around their tiny TV and support the Cuban boxer, one of many Cubans competing in the Summer Olympics in London. As it turned out, he was not competing quite yet, so we headed out to the caves. This was a good thing, because it was getting fairly late in the day, and it was best to go as soon as possible in order to avoid walking through the jungle at night.

The grandson of the house undertook to be our guide, He took us down a series of makeshift ladders, down the face of a bunch of caves until we ultimately dropped into the jungle. From there, it was another five-minute walk to a cave that was just wide enough for us to climb in and descend thirty meters to where the salt water emerged from the rocks and up into the cave. The depth and height of the water was contingent upon the ocean's tides, as the water that we swam in at the bottom of this cave came directly from the ocean through a series of underground labyrinths and channels. Our guide, whose name I couldn't remember, brought a homemade lantern so that we could see as we descended into the cave to have a swim.

All of these cave systems were created by the movement of plate tectonics and lava that, over time, created all of these cave structures and underwater caves that more than likely ran underneath most of Cuba. And now, its beauty was here for all to discover and appreciate. When I asked our guide how he found this place, because it was hidden in the middle of nowhere, he told me that his great-grandfather had been looking for firewood one day when he stumbled upon it. From that point on, it became an escape for the handful of locals who lived there. Now it's become a tourist attraction for those who are willing to make the approximately five-mile round-trip journey from the center of Baracoa to the cave and back. Moreover, the State has capitalized on this attraction by charging tourists to go there. However, since we decided to go after the guard had gone home, we were given the tour by the finders of the cave.

As we were walking to and from the cave, I noticed that our guide was walking in what appeared to be women's sandals which, additionally, were broken, with an opening in the front part of his shoe. So not only were they a bit small and uncomfortable looking, but they were also falling apart. And for good reason. Having to walk out in the jungle for most of the day, every day, would be taxing on any pair of sandals. So I thought to myself, *How can I offer him my shoes without making a big deal about it in front of his family?* I waited until we got back from the trek to the cave and after we had paid him for taking us to the cave to make the switch. He actually told us just to give the money to his grandfather, who needed the money to pay for his Parkinson's medicine, which cost $2 a month. After I gave the money to his grandfather, I casually tried on his sandals to make sure that we had the same size foot. Then I told him to "check out my sandals."

It was obvious that he liked them. With a big smile, he said, "These are nice!" And they fit him perfectly. So I said, "Let's trade!" I think that he thought that I was crazy. So I just kept his sandals on, said good-bye to the family, and Katie, Carmen, and I headed home, which was over two and a half miles away. After walking for about one hundred meters, I told Carmen and Katie that I had no idea how our guide had been able to walk in these sandals, because aside from how uncomfortable they were, I couldn't figure out how his feet fit inside his old sandals. His feet were wider than mine, and I was having trouble squeezing my feet into those sandals. At least I knew that I had another pair of shoes in my *casa*. So I bit the bullet and made the long trek home in the most uncomfortable shoes that I had ever worn. In fact, I would have walked barefoot, but there were too many sharp rocks and shells to risk it.

Instead of focusing on the pain of walking in these shoes, I distracted myself for most of the walk by thinking about how the "backwoods" of Baracoa seemed like something out of an old Cuban movie: mountains covered with palm trees and banana plants, fruit trees hanging over the trail, people riding on ox carts, and so on. It seemed as though all that was missing was a guy in a white *guyabera* (a typical Cuban shirt) and linen pants smoking a cigar in a tobacco field. And as luck would have it, he appeared. Out of nowhere appeared a guy, sitting on an ox cart with no shirt on and smoking a cigar. There was just something about the ambience that seemed so apropos. Even though the walk back home was long and tiresome, I couldn't help but enjoy the beauty of the Cuban countryside that accompanied us on our way home.

During the trip, I was able to talk with Carmen and Katie about a number of issues that were on my mind concerning the Cuban system, specifically pertaining to Baracoa. For example, Katie and I found out that there were places where tourists weren't allowed to go. The Tourism Police said that tourists couldn't go to these places for their own safety since they did not have the infrastructure to protect the tourists.[32] This doesn't apply specifically to theft; rather, it applies to accidents and other mishaps. I was surprised to find that these places were considered off-limits for tourists. My first thought was to assume that these were places that the government was trying to keep out of sight from the tourists so that they didn't see the "reality" of the situation here. Yet, after walking around and seeing that even in the "safe" places there were elements of poverty, I realized that the places that were off-limits couldn't be any better or worse than the places that we, as tourists, could visit. It was clearly not that they were trying to keep the tourists away from the locals, as I was able to walk through Baracoa and its local community *en route* to *La Cueva de Paraíso*. And during that walk, I was able to gain real insight into how many Cubans in Baracoa lived in their day-to-day lives. As we strolled through the non-touristy parts of Baracoa where most of the locals lived, no one ever asked us to turn around or told us that it was off-limits. And we were able to visit many locations where we could have had an accident or mishap. So after talking with Katie and getting her insight and her opinion on the matter, we came to the conclusion that it may be a policy that really makes no sense. However, since no one had questioned it before, it remains as it is. It was unfortunate, because this rule kept us from going to eat a Baracoian-style dinner at Carmen's father's house; his house was in an area that was deemed "off-limits" for tourists.

The more I traveled around Cuba and began to digest all that I had seen across the country, I couldn't help but become more and more intrigued by their system. At the same time, and to my dismay, I found myself becoming more and more critical of the system as well, because it did, from my perspective, sometimes seem as though the Tourism Police were trying to segregate the locals from the tourists. And for someone who wants to integrate into the Cuban society, this poses a problem.

At the same time, in trying to stay objective, I reminded myself that it also keeps both the tourists and the locals "safe." In other countries, particularly in the developing world, when the local population and the tourists integrate with one another, there is a higher level of theft and other petty crimes that accompany this interaction. I am not suggesting that the Cuban people are given to theft or are dangerous; however, this situation may be something that the Cuban government is making an effort to avoid. I guess that you could say that they are just trying to protect their "investment," that is, the tourist. On the other hand, my friend Carmen, in an attempt to alleviate my cynicism, offered a logical rebuttal to my hypothesis by suggesting that "Not all tourists have good intentions, and perhaps, especially since Cuba has been targeted for attacks by Cuban-Americans and other entities that dislike the current government, keeping the tourists away from certain areas also protects the Cubans from any incidents that could endanger their lives." Whether or not I saw the reason or benefit, it was a rule that was presumably put in place for some reason, and therefore, as a tourist, I must respect it whether I agreed with it or not.

I had the opportunity to speak with some people out in the countryside near the cave about another government policy that seemed a bit peculiar to me. In the outskirts of Baracoa, there seemed to be an excess of fruit; there was literally more fruit lying around than there were people to eat it. So naturally, one's first inclination, albeit a bit capitalist in nature, would be to bag it up, take it to the center of town where there was less fruit, and sell it to people. That would sound like a good idea even if you weren't a capitalist, as it would be a great way to supplement your income. But unfortunately for the residents in this community, not only did the government trucks not come out there to purchase fruit—they claim that it's too hard to get to, and thus, not cost effective—but they wouldn't even allow the locals to sell their own fruit without a permit. In other words, the only people who had permission to sell fruit were either the people with a permit, or the government. This would not be as strange if the government were to send people out to collect and buy this fruit so that it didn't go to waste. However, the fruit just fell to the ground and rotted, because the locals were prohibited from selling it to anyone. If these residents did try to sell the fruit in the streets of Baracoa—which many of them illegally tried to do—they were fined by the government.

I completely understand the concept behind the law, which is to control who sells what. Thus the tax, which is paid by the individuals who have a permit, and subsequently given to the government, is then redistributed, or reallocated, in order to meet the needs of the people on a larger, more communal scale. The revenue from the tax, in theory, is used by the State to subsidize the cost of education, health care, etc., for all citizens. This is one manifestation of what is known as the redistribution of wealth, which is a key element in the socialist system. However, to me it was baffling that these individuals couldn't sell small amounts of leftover fruit to the community in order to make a few extra Cuban pesos to supplement their income. This was an example of one of the policies, particularly in Baracoa, that didn't make a lot of sense to me. I was unable to get any legitimate justification, or explanation, regarding some of these policies, and I would imagine that, as a citizen, it could at times seem nearly impossible to get ahead.

Still, in defense of the government, the taxes are intended to be reallocated back into the Cuban society. That is how the system works. Supplying benefits like health care and education depends upon the taxes that are paid by the people. And the money earned from tourism is essentially what sustains Cuba as a nation. It is important to see that the middle class in the U.S., by way of taxation, also helps to sustain and perpetuate the U.S. system. So the theoretical principle behind controlling tax dollars so they can be used to perpetuate a particular system of government, whether in Cuba or the U.S., is essentially the same concept.

Since Cuba is a socialist country, the government controls approximately 90 percent of all the businesses (individuals have only recently been able to start their own business), which in addition to their ambitious plan of supplying all citizens with basic amenities, means that the government has a huge burden to bear. Under a socialist system, the government is the one who owns, operates, and controls essentially everything. That is the socialist model which, in Cuba, is precisely the model that the revolution has sought to realize. And yet, despite being a country with little to no natural resources and a relatively low GDP, they have managed to keep this ideology intact for over fifty-three years. Recently, Cuba has been loosening up a bit in terms of its governmental micromanagement, which has allowed for private business, such as the privately-owned taxis, the *casa particulars,* and privately-owned restaurants, to flourish within the Cuban socialist system.

STILL IN BARACOA

I had the opportunity to go with Katie, Carmen, her brother Papito, and the rest of their family in Baracoa to *Playa Maguana* where Papito's wife, Carla, grew up. This was a day trip that we had been planning for a few days, as it was Papito's only day off this week. Katie and I had planned to leave Baracoa the following day, so we decided that this would be a good day to have a going-away party on the beach. It also seemed like a great way to get all of the family out for a day, outside of town at the beach.

After loading up all ten of us, including the driver, into an old Willys truck, we took off for *Playa Maguana*. The truck had been converted into a taxi, which meant that our driver had replaced the seats with comfortable benches in the cargo area of the truck. I use the term *comfortable* in a relative sense; still, it was not a bad ride, except for the fact that the truck kept stalling out on the way there and again on the way back. There seemed to be a short circuit in the ignition, because the horn also decided to honk at inopportune times as well. This kind of random vehicle behavior was pretty common in Cuba. So no one else really thought much of the truck cutting out on us every few miles.

Playa Maguana was an extremely beautiful coastal area with pictur-esque beaches, turquoise waters, and a beautiful reef just off the shore. I sometimes felt as though I was becoming accustomed to the beauty of Cuba; however, just when I thought that I was inured to it all, Cuba always managed to pull another unique experience out of its bag of tricks. This time, it was in the form of a little, white spiky sea creature that we all know as the sea urchin.

But before I was taught something new by the Cubans, I had to eat lunch.

This, by no means, was a typical lunch, as we cooked a pig, fried plantains, and made rice and beans, and then ate all of it under the palm trees on the sand at the beach. I had the good fortune of being part of two pig roasts during my travels across Cuba: this one at *Playa Maguana* in Baracoa, and the other one with the group of friends at the beach near Levisa, in Holguín. What made those cookouts so special was that each time I was able to help my friends afford to take their whole family out to enjoy some quality time together at a place they rarely got to visit. In the case of *Playa Maguana,* it was a tourist beach and was also a bit far from Baracoa for locals to rent a truck at $20 per roundtrip. So to get the opportunity to come to a beach like *Playa Maguana* with their entire family made for an exceptional day, as it was a rare occurrence for them.

After lunch, I spent time with Papito's wife's brother and joked about picking up the sea urchins that were out in the water all around the reefs. He told me that the white sea urchins make a great urchin cocktail. This to me was not only intriguing, but it sounded like a lot of fun. So I told him, still joking, that we should go out and catch some and make a cocktail. And as soon I said it, he told me to get my snorkeling mask and we would go grab about forty to fifty of them from the reefs and make sea urchin cocktails for everyone. Naturally, I didn't hesitate; however, I was a bit concerned that we were doing something illegal. So I asked him if we were allowed to go out into the reefs and fish out the urchins—who were in the hundreds and seemed to be taking over the reefs—and he told me that he had a fishing license, and therefore, we were legally able to go do what I had jokingly suggested. It was a bit too late to back out, so I was very relieved when he told me that it was totally legal. If it hadn't been, I myself would not have gotten into any trouble; however, he would have been heavily fined by the police if we were caught. Luckily for us, he did have one, so off we went, down the beach and into the water.

As we were on our way to go fishing for the sea urchins, I asked him how much he paid to get a fishing license. He told me that he had to pay the State one hundred Cuban pesos a year, which is the equivalent of $4 a year. I was astounded at how cheap getting a fishing license was. It struck me as almost too cheap, compared with what other people paid for licenses—for instance a taxi license costs $50 per month—because a fisherman who fishes for urchins, lobsters, red snapper, and other seafood, can make good money selling them to the local hotels, as well as to tourists. I told him that I should move to Cuba to get a fishing license so that I could work with him.

This short conversation showed me that, even though the State controlled who fished these waters, the cost for a license was extremely affordable, especially when one takes into account the money that a fisherman could make if he or she were good at it. The only difficulty, according to my friend, was that it was hard for him to replace the bands that were on his spear gun. They were virtually nonexistent in Cuba, and therefore, extremely difficult to get. That made fishing a bit challenging at times, as he relied on his spear gun for catching fish and lobsters. So equipment problems could perhaps be one of the only drawbacks to being a fisherman. Furthermore, if his flippers were to break, he wouldn't be able to just buy a new pair, as they were not readily available; he would have to sew them up. Still, as far as I was concerned, those appeared to be minor details compared to the fun he was having being out in the water and fishing, and the potential income he could make from it. And his son fished with him as well, which meant that they could make twice the amount of money on one license. According to what he told me, his son was still able to fish with his license since he was still under eighteen years old.

Once we were in the water, the reef was right there, and the water was full of sea urchins. We wasted no time grabbing them and throwing them into the sack that we had brought with us. I didn't have a snorkel, so I had to hold my breath and go underwater to get them. Although it was only two meters deep at its deepest, it was still a bit difficult, as the waves were washing me up and over the reef at times. My fisherman friend had no problem grabbing two urchins at a time. Me, I was only able to grab one at a time.

I knew from previous experience the correct way to grab them in order to avoid being shot with their toxins. Yet I had to be careful as I pulled them from the reef. I am typically not one to do this type of reef fishing; however, given that these urchins were taking over the reef, and that my friend and his son were the only two who appeared to fish this area, I was okay with grabbing a few urchins to make a cocktail. In fact, he often does this to sell them to the tourists. He told me that he sells a sea urchin cocktail for approximately $7 a cup. And with the amount that we grabbed, we could have made about eight cups of sea urchin cocktails. So I jokingly said that we lost over $50 by not selling them. Then he suggested that I come back the following day, and we would do the same thing, and instead of giving them to our friends, we would sell them to the tourists. And since I could speak English—he only spoke Spanish—we would have no problem selling them. I doubt it would have been a problem even if he didn't speak English, as these cocktails would be considered delicacies in Europe and North America. So I imagine that the tourists would have been happy to pay $7 for a cocktail, and not too bothered by figuring out how to communicate that. And with good reason: they were fresh, and extremely tasty.

As we were packing up to leave the beach, my friend's nephew came up with a gigantic lobster, which was one of three that he had just caught out in the reef. I told him that if he were to sell that lobster tail that he just caught, then he would earn enough money to pay for his license for another year. Of course they thought that was funny, even though they also knew that it was true. But in the true community spirit of Cuba, he gave it to Papito's wife, Carla, who was also his aunt.

This was well received. It was no small gift, because average Cubans don't get to indulge themselves in food like lobster, as it was a delicacy reserved for the tourists and, in addition, was not within the budgets of most Cubans. So it was very much appreciated to have a gigantic lobster tail to cook up for dinner. As we were leaving, Carla's brother, the one who took me fishing for sea urchins, and her nephew told me again that I should come back so that we could go out and get more urchins and lobsters to sell to the tourists. And as I hugged them and said "Good-bye," I told them that if my plans were to change and I were to decide to stay longer in Baracoa, then I would certainly take them up on their offer. This did not happen, because I had to get to Santiago de Cuba, but I very much appreciated their words and their hospitality.

Another thought that came to mind as I was talking with my friends Katie and Carmen that day—not that I was noticing it for the first time—was that Cuba seemed to be stuck in the past. In some ways, that wasn't a bad thing; for instance, the 1950s cars were wonderful. But in other ways, it seemed that they were still basking in the revolution to such an extent that they had failed to develop much over the past fifty-three years. I have highlighted the socialist billboards, signs, and overall propaganda that was sprinkled across all of Cuba. And even though I agree that it creates a sense of solidarity among the people, I felt as though it had prevented Cuba from progressing. I concur that the Cuban Revolution was not only a historic achievement, but it also brought about a system that gave many Cubans who were otherwise marginalized a chance to become doctors, lawyers, professors, etc. So while I consider that achievement to be a good thing for the overall Cuban society, I still felt that Cuba had essentially put the emergency brake on its own development since the revolution, and had therefore spent way too much time congratulating itself on the fifty-three-year-long "victory of ideas," as some of the billboards suggested. Much of this, perhaps, could be attributed to the United States' economic blockade on Cuba that began in the early 1960s.

Still, one can only speculate about who or what is responsible for Cuba's lack of development over the last fifty-three years. I would argue that there are multiple causes, not the least of which is the U.S. trade embargo. However, the fall of the Soviet Union and other subsequent crises have certainly contributed to the stagnation of progress in Cuba.

Moreover, I am not suggesting that Cuba adopt the model of the United States, or of any other capitalist nation for that matter; but I think it would do Cuba good to catch up with technologies such as the Internet, or even international tourism standards that seem to be lacking in most places on this beautiful island. Cuba already has the conditions to be a world-class location for tourists. And to a certain degree, it is already that; however, it lacks some basic elements that would allow this country to integrate into the world tourism market as a high-profile tourist destination. To me, Cuba is one of the most beautiful countries that I have seen in the Caribbean. Its size lends itself to beautiful landscapes, rivers, high mountains, and cultural diversity, which not all Caribbean islands can boast.

Still, Cuba lacks basic tools such as websites for promoting their beautiful resorts. In fact, the local people by and large didn't even have access to the Internet to create a website, or promote their *casa particular*. Most of the hotels were run by Gaviota, a State-run tourism company. They were the only company that oversaw and built nearly all of the hotels found in Cuba. They also ran other tourist excursions, such as boat trips and diving. And even though I didn't necessarily see that as a bad thing, I think that in order for Gaviota to create a strong tourism business in Cuba, they need to promote what they are doing to the outside world much more effectively. It would also help if the managers and other employees that work at these facilities had access to the Internet and other worldwide systems of communication so that they could see what else is out there, and improve on what they were already doing in order to make their services that much better—a sort of "best practices" exchange. This would be a great way to increase traffic to some of these remote hotels like Hotel Maguana, which was an extremely amazing eco-lodge that had breathtaking views and a beautiful beach just in front of the hotel. But when I was at Hotel Maguana, it was practically empty of guests. I told Carmen that it was apparent that this place didn't promote itself properly, because there is no way that somewhere like this should ever be empty, particularly during Cuba's high season.

It seemed to me that in these ways, Cuba was stuck in the past and had isolated itself from the developing world by resisting any form of progress, thereby preventing it from reaching its maximum potential as a tourist destination. I believe this could be done without having Cuba drop its socialist model; without giving up their ideology, they could open themselves up a bit more to the rest of the world in order to upgrade their services. This, in turn, would not only connect the Cuban people more with the rest of the world, but it would also make them a strong competitor in the world's market for international tourism. I don't want to downplay Cuba's already-existing popularity as a travel destination; however, how, as a tourist, do you find a listing for *all* the hotels and not just the ones at Varadero Beach? What if you are a businessman or businesswoman on vacation and you need to use the Internet for work while you are staying at a beautiful ocean-front resort such as Hotel Maguana? Must you hire a taxi driver to take you into downtown Baracoa—a forty-minute drive on bumpy roads—for $20 for the privilege of paying $6 an hour for Internet? More likely, you would choose to go to somewhere else in the Caribbean to stay in a more up-to-date and internationally connected hotel. That way, you can enjoy your vacation and also get some work done, so that your business does not fall apart in your absence.

Far from suggesting that Cuba make any huge changes to their socialist ideology, I would humbly suggest that they move past the attack at the Moncada Barracks (July 26, 1953) and the Cuban Revolution (January 1, 1959) and begin to live in the twenty-first century. The Cuban people and their history are such a beautiful part of who they are that it is not something that should be forgotten; but it would be nice to see this beautiful island reach its full potential with regard to tourism, for the sake of the Cuban people, as well as the Cuban government. Because at the end of the day, that is one of their primary ways of providing income to the island. It's in their best interest in order to continue to sustainably perpetuate their socialist ideology by seeking out ways of using technology to promote Cuba's beauty. This is quite different from suggesting that Cuba sell out, or be exploited by the imperialist powers around the world. I would just like to see Cuba take better measures to promote themselves, so that more people can come and experience the Cuban way of life in many of the same ways that I was able to experience it.

SANTIAGO DE CUBA

After getting to Santiago de Cuba after a five-and-a-half-hour bus ride from Baracoa, my friend Katie and I planned out the next couple days, in which we would walk around *el centro*, or the downtown, of Santiago and visit some of the historic buildings in Cuba. Then the following day, we were going to go to a place called *La Gran Piedra* ("The Big Rock"), which turned out to be nothing more than a rock outcropping that stuck out above the mountains. Yet, the views from the top of the four-hundred-plus stairs that led up to it were breathtaking. In fact, the cool breeze can be a bit breathtaking too, if you go too early in the morning. So allowing ourselves the luxury of killing two birds with one stone—sleeping in and not freezing at the top of the big rock—we decided to start our day trip around 12:00 p.m.

Walking around Santiago was certainly interesting, as it was the first time in quite a while that I had been back in a big city in Cuba. So going from Baracoa, which was extremely rural and natural, to one of the biggest cities in Cuba, was a bit overwhelming. I felt overpowered by all of the traffic, the exhaust from the cars, and the number and size of the buildings. I also missed being near the beach and the waterfalls, and all the other natural attractions. Nevertheless, Santiago was a must-see on my list, if only to visit the Moncada Barracks, which was where the first uprising against Batista's government took place. While it was a relatively feeble attempt to mount a *coup d'etat* against one of Batista's largest military barracks, and was quickly stomped out by Batista's men, it nonetheless marked a historical moment for Fidel Castro, as it served as the catalyst that led to the Cuban Revolution. And the rest, as they say, is history—remembering that *"history"* was part of the name of

Castro's book, *History Will Absolve Me*, which he wrote after being imprisoned for his part in the Moncada attack.

However, instead of going straight to Moncada, I decided to let that be the grand finale, the last thing I would see after walking through the entire downtown historical district of Santiago. So Katie and I started at the *Plaza de la Revolución*, which was right next to our *casa* and the Viazul bus terminal. From there, we took a bike taxi (*bici-taxi*) into the city in order to start at the *Museo de la Lucha Clandestina* ("Museum of the Clandestine Fight"). Unfortunately, when we got there, we realized that it was Monday, which meant that not only was this museum closed, but others would be closed as well. And since Monday was really the only day we had for walking around town, this meant that we would not be able to go inside some of these buildings. Apparently, for most of Cuba, if not all of Cuba, Monday appeared to be what Sunday is in the United States, in terms of it being a "day of rest." Nevertheless, we decided to walk around and check out whatever might be open. Actually, Katie had already been to Santiago with Maria, another one of our friends; however, she hadn't been able to walk around and see the sights. So it worked out perfectly for her that she was able to come back, not to mention that sharing the cost of taxis and *casas* was helpful for both of us.

So after walking around for a while, I made the suggestion that we take a coffee break in the *Parque Céspedes*. *Céspedes* is the last name of Carlos Manuel de Céspedes, the first president of the Cuba after its independence from Spain. He was to Cuba what George Washington was to the United States, and just as popular with Cubans as Washington is with Americans. There is even a quote by Fidel Castro in Céspedes' house in Bayamo that reads, "The only revolution that has ever existed in Cuba is Céspedes' revolution, and we are just carrying the torch for now."

We decided to go to, as Katie put it, a posh hotel (she is British, and *posh* means upscale) and get our coffee there. Actually Katie drank tea because she is not a fan of coffee. Nevertheless, it was a great place to hang out and people-watch for about an hour before continuing on with our improvised tour around Santiago. It also promised to work out well for Katie to check at the Viazul Information Center about her ticket to Trinidad, but unfortunately the phone lines were down, and as a result, she couldn't get any information after all. However, she was extremely relaxed about this minor inconvenience, as she had been in Cuba long enough to know that something like that wasn't unusual. The Viazul bus line was an extremely nice bus line; nonetheless, they apparently don't use the Internet to sell bus tickets; you have to physically go to the bus station to purchase your ticket. Even in Havana and Santiago, which are the largest hubs for the bus line, you have to show up in person to see if there is space. And even in Santiago and Havana, it was tough to get accurate information from the information centers, because occasionally the phone lines were down or the Viazul employee was out to lunch.

Just before we left *Parque Céspedes*, a random Cuban showed up just outside of the *terraza* of the hotel and decided that he would entertain everyone by yelling at the top of his lungs something that sounded like a long drawn-out "Papaaaaaa!" (*papá* means "dad" in Spanish) with a strange cackle at the end. He would yell it and would draw it out for about five to ten seconds. I thought it was hilarious; however, I don't think everyone felt the same about it as I did. And given that he was in his forties or fifties, I am sure his *papá* was not around there, and that he was just trying to be annoying and disturb the guests on the terrace of the hotel restaurant. After listening to him yell/sing for about ten minutes, we left and continued on toward Moncada. And finally, once we got to Moncada, it was closed, not that this came as a surprise. Nevertheless, we were still able to walk around the outside, take pictures of the building, and check out the bullet holes that remained inside the walls of these barracks, now a museum named "The 26th of July" after the date of the attack in 1953. For me, the visit to the Moncada Barracks was extremely significant to me in terms of my field work and my study of Cuba and its revolution. It, like the Che mausoleum, is a significant landmark, both literal and figurative, that stands as a testament to the revolution and its ideology.

Even in the presence of such an historic monument, there were kids in the empty field in front of *el Cuartel Moncada* playing soccer. It was an interesting juxtaposition of energies that left me at a loss for words. On the one hand, the young generation of Cubans were playing soccer in the yard of a building that once witnessed one of the most historic uprisings against Batista. And on the other hand, there stands a building riddled with bullet holes from another generation of youngsters who left their mark on this place over fifty years ago. Interestingly enough, had the revolution not turned out to be a success, which might well have happened, since victory was won against great odds, then the attack on Moncada would have gone down in history as one of the biggest blunders in Cuban history. But given the fascination people around the world have with Cuba, and the iconization of both Fidel and Che Guevara, it appears that history will indeed absolve Fidel Castro, as he predicted.

After walking around and checking out downtown Santiago de Cuba, Katie and I decided that it would be a good idea to head back to the *casa* to get some dinner and ask our family about a fun place to go out after dinner. From what we had been told, Santiago de Cuba was a city that was known for its *vida nocturna* ("nightlife"), as it was famous for having great musicians that performed through the early morning hours. The music, of course, was accompanied by lots of people dancing salsa and just enjoying a night out on the town. However, before dinner, we got into a provocative conversation with the owners of the *casa*. We were talking about the current Cuban government, Cuban family members living in the United States, and their overall satisfaction—or, more specifically, the lack thereof—with the current system in Cuba. This was one of the first times that a family as a whole was complaining to me about the system. Even so, most of the complaints were nothing new to me, as these same complaints were recurring themes and conversation topics across the country. Generally, it was an individual who voiced these concerns, but in this case, it was the whole family who sat down with us to vent their frustrations towards the Cuban government.

They complained, as did many others, about low wages, about how it was impossible for a typical Cuban to get a visa and passport to travel, and that the cost of living continued to rise while wages stayed the same. In some instances, even the locals had to pay in CUC (Cuban convertible pesos, the tourist currency) for day-to-day items and even some medicines. They talked with much resentment toward the situation in which they were living, even though they were actually living pretty well. They had a two-story house with a fenced-in terrace up on top. And from what I had gathered, the only work they were doing was running their *casa particular*, which was set up to hold two guests, as they had two rooms available in their house.

After this conversation with our hosts, Katie and I tried to figure out where the bulk of their income was coming from. They didn't seem to be a house that hosted a ton of tourists. Still, whether they had guests or not, they had to pay the State $300 a month in taxes for having two rooms for rent. My host had told us that was the tax for having a *casa particular* in Santiago de Cuba, as the tax on a *casa particular* varied from city to city. This meant that if they had both rooms full at $15 a night (total of $30) for only half of the month, or approximately two weeks, then they would make just enough to cover the tax that the government levied on them. That meant that there wouldn't even be enough money for them to live on. And having two rooms occupied for half a month, every month of the year, was not an easy task, especially when there are other *casas* much closer to downtown Santiago de Cuba. To us, it seemed that in terms of the *casa particular* options, the supply outweighed the demand; however, that was only my perception, as I was unable to get any empirical data to support that observation.

This was the second time that Katie and I had stood in for the government as a verbal punching bag that day. Before even getting back to the *casa*, we had been approached by a *jinetero*, or Cuban male escort, who asked me if I knew about the *real* Cuba. I told him that I was aware of the realities here; however, as Katie put it, I was very diplomatic with my answer, as I had no clue who this guy was and why he wanted to talk to us about the *real* Cuba. In many cases, there are government officials who dress in street clothes and walk around to listen to people. So having that in mind, I was very careful with my choice of words when I answered his loaded questions. In fact, after the conversation, which lasted much longer than I had wanted, Katie congratulated me on successfully replying to all of his questions without actually answering any of them.

After being assaulted with loaded questions and controversial conversations—not that I am ordinarily opposed to either—we decided that we would go to *La Casa de la Trova* in downtown Santiago de Cuba. We had walked around there all day, so we were both familiar with where to go. *La Casa de la Trova* is a government-run "franchise," much like *La Casa de la Música*. The quotes are put there because "franchise" is a capitalist word that the Cuban people do not use; however, *La Casa de la Trova* certainly meets the requirements for being a franchise, except that it is government-run. It is famous for great music and an all-around great setting for tourists and locals alike. So we went there and enjoyed some terrific music and watched some awe-inspiring dancing. It was a place that had such a great vibe and such great music that it even evoked in me the desire to get up and dance. However, dancing with Katie reminded me how bad of a salsa dancer I am. Nevertheless, I couldn't resist trying. I'm sure I should blame the urge to dance on the great music.

It also reminded me of an e-mail that I received while in Cuba, from a good Colombian friend of mine who lives in Tampa, where she told me that she hoped I would return from Cuba "dancing like a Cuban." I reassured my Colombian friend that I would "return" from Cuba; however, I would certainly not come back dancing like a Cuban. They are such amazing dancers and seem to just flow with the music, an element of dancing that I cannot seem to grasp. In fact, many times I tell people that I am Latino off the dance floor, but that on the dance floor I am *gringo*, implying that I am not a good dancer, which is something that Latinos, particularly Caribbean Latinos, are known for. It's a stereotype for sure, but it's generally true, perhaps because people learn to dance as children, and it is a larger part of their daily lives. Even for a *gringo* dancer, *La Casa de la Trova* was a great place to spend one of only two nights in Santiago. It gave me a flavor of Santiago de Cuba that I was not able to get during the day.

After helping the wait-staff close down *La Casa de la Trova*, I got a good night's sleep. The following day, I went with Katie and two of our hosts to the place called *La Gran Piedra*, which I mentioned before. Even though it was basically just a rock outcropping that jutted out from the mountainside, the view from the top, approximately 1,300 meters above sea level, was spectacular. Climbing *el Yunque* a few days prior made the staircase that we took to the top of *La Gran Piedra* (450-plus steps) seem like a walk in the park. I guess technically it *was* a walk in the park, because *La Gran Piedra* is part of a larger set of sites and parks in this part of the province.

Just a bit down from the Rock was a *hacienda*, or plantation, that was put there by a rich Haitian plantation owner who left Haiti in the late eighteenth century to escape the Haitian Revolt. Interestingly enough, the Haitian Revolt was the first slave revolt in the New World, which directly led to Haiti's independence from France on January 1, 1804, after fighting the Haitian revolution for over 12 years, since 1791. This *hacienda* was one of a handful of its kind responsible for introducing the coffee industry to Cuba.

These plantations, which once housed slaves as well (the unfortunate ones who were brought over by the owners as they were escaping from the rebel slaves in Haiti), were the first places to produce coffee in Cuba. Now they stand strong as evidence of a part of Cuban—and Haitian—history. They now serve as museums where people can learn about the French-Haitians and their slaves in Cuba, and the beginning of the Cuban coffee industry, which was still going strong over two hundred years later. One of the most interesting parts of the tour wasn't even the *hacienda* itself, but rather the fact that the people in charge of the museum charged us one CUC (equivalent to $1); however, if we wanted to take pictures, which was what most people like to do when they visit museums, then we would have to pay five CUC more ($5). This brought up an interesting conversation between Katie and me as we rode home in the back of our taxi, a 1970s Willys Jeep.

There was a pervasive capitalist system running parallel to the Cuban socialist system. As I have already mentioned, there are two monetary systems in Cuba: the Cuban national peso, which is the Cuban national currency; and the Cuban convertible peso, which is the tourist currency also known as the CUC, or *Chavito*. That in itself is intriguing. Normally countries in the Caribbean and Central America allow the use of the dollar in their country, which would lead one to think that there are unofficially two currencies; however, in Cuba, there is a currency for the locals and a currency for the tourists, which makes many things unattainable for the locals, simply for the fact that a working professional makes no more than $70 (many make only around $15–$30) a month working as an employee of the State. So capitalizing on tourist dollars in itself is a form of capitalism, which seemed a bit ironic in a place that staunchly opposed capitalism. (Or perhaps, the State staunchly opposed competition, and was happy being the only capitalist in Cuba.) It seems nearly impossible to have a tourism industry in a country—even a country like Cuba—and not have a form of capitalism. In fact, it is quite impossible for anyone to avoid capitalism completely. The only way to completely avoid capitalism would be to never buy anything and just run around naked in the jungle and live your life as if the outside world isn't even there. Because the moment you buy the basic items necessary for survival, such as clothes, toiletries, or groceries, you have fallen victim to consumerism, and thus, capitalism. So to claim to be a country utterly free of capitalism would be impossible, just as you can't be totally free of socialism if you want to build roads and public schools and police departments, and so on.

Furthermore, it could be said that Cuba is full of capitalism. One example of this—and there are many—are the people in the streets selling the national three-peso bill to tourists. This bill happens to be a bill coveted by tourists, as it has Che Guevara's face on it. Remember: it takes twenty-five national pesos to make one CUC, yet the people selling these "Che" bills sold them to naive tourists for one CUC. Thus, they made a profit of twenty-two national pesos every time they sold one of these bills to a tourist. And just to put this into perspective, if they were to sell twenty "Che" bills, for example, they would make more doing that than the average State employee makes in his or her job. Consider that a physical therapist in Cuba makes approximately $15 a month. And if these opportunists were to pick a place where the demand was high—for example, *Havana Vieja*—then they could potentially make even more. In my humble opinion, that is capitalism. Of course one could say that the State was not participating in that, and the person saying that would be right; but the State had its own ways of using capitalism to its advantage, like charging five CUC above the entrance fee for anyone who wanted to take pictures in the museum. That extra $5 was money that went back to the State.

Another example was the exchange rate between the CUC and the U.S. dollar—or any other currency, for that matter. Cuba claimed that the exchange rate between the USD and the CUC was one-to-one (that is, one U.S. dollar for one CUC); however, that is a bit misleading because when a tourist goes to the bank or CADECA (money exchange company), they charge him or her 13 percent to exchange U.S. dollars for CUC. In other words, if you give the bank teller 100 U.S. dollars, the teller will give you back 87 CUC. They call this a tariff, but no matter how you look at it, that makes the exchange rate less than one to one. This is not necessarily a critique of the system; I am merely suggesting that these tactics appear to be subtle forms of capitalism cleverly integrated by the State into the Cuban system in order to "justifiably" extort more money out of the tourist. And the most interesting thing is that even though Cuba claims to peg the CUC to the U.S. dollar, the CUC is worthless anywhere outside of Cuba. It was a currency created by the government only for tourists to use within Cuba, and which had a twenty-five-to-one exchange rate with the Cuban national peso (twenty-five national pesos for one CUC).

Finally, I was told by a taxi driver in Holguín, who has since become a friend of mine, that when I was in Holguín on my last trip, I paid thirty CUC for him to take me to the beach because the proprietor of the *casa* took five CUC and gave him twenty-five. Twenty-five CUC is all he charges; however, the *casa* owner took her percentage out as a "referral fee." I was actually a bit perturbed when he told me this. It made me happy that I did not go back to stay in that same *casa particular,* as they clearly were taking advantage of a new tourist. Interestingly enough, I saw more money-hungry people in a country that claims to not care about money than I had in most of my travels across Latin America. I am not saying that people do not overcharge and do things like that elsewhere; however, it is expected in a capitalist-minded society as just another way to make money. In fact, many tourist just see it as a "*gringo* tax."

But seeing those types of tactics in action in a theoretically "communalistic" country like Cuba caught me off guard. I found it a bit ironic that these capitalist tactics seem to come naturally, despite the fact that these same individuals are taught that capitalism is bad and socialism is good.

These are just a few small examples of capitalism that I noted while traveling around Cuba. This doesn't even take into account the largest "export" that Cuba has, which was selling Che Guevara T-shirts, paraphernalia, and anything else that they could put his iconic face on. In short, I am not bringing awareness to this as a way to critique Cuba's approach to capitalism. In fact, it is quite the contrary. I have suggested that Cuba would benefit from injecting a bit more capitalism into their system in order to bring more revenue into the country. This would ultimately help to financially support the current Cuban socialist model, and thereby perpetuate Cuba's sociopolitical ideology as a whole. In fact, one could make the assertion that in the end, it would increase the revenue available to redistribute among the Cuban people.

AVOIDING CHOLERA
IN BAYAMO

After a few days in Santiago, it was time to continue moving toward Holguín so that I could make it back with a little time to spend with my friends before flying back to the United States. However, Katie and I decided that it would be a good idea to make a pit stop in Bayamo *en route* to Holguín. Although I was going to Holguín, Katie was continuing to Trinidad, Havana, and Viñales before returning to England. Even though we heard that there were numerous cases of cholera in Bayamo (and Manzanillo), we decided that it wouldn't be a problem as long as we didn't drink any water, or eat anything that may have been washed with the tap water. If we stuck to those simple rules, then we would greatly reduce our chances of getting cholera, as the bacterium *Vibrio cholerae* is transmitted only through water, or the fecal matter of an infected person. The one other way that it can get into a community is through seafood such as fish and lobster. It attaches itself to the fish or lobster, and is transmitted to the person upon consumption of the contaminated food. Then it can be spread through the septic system through human waste and through aqueducts.

That was the case in Haiti after the 2010 earthquake shook the Haitian capital city of Port-au-Prince nearly to the ground. The water systems and other utilities were so badly contaminated with the bacterium that they were not able to put a stop to the epidemic, and it just continued to spread and infect more and more people, ultimately killing thousands. Many of the people who died from cholera were either the elderly or young children who, sadly, did not have a strong-enough immune system to fight off the bacteria. They usually died from dehydration or some other cause associated with extreme loss of bodily fluids.

The situation with cholera in Cuba was by no means what it was in Haiti after the earthquake. In fact, as soon as it began to spread, the Cuban government moved to get it under control. They were able to detect the source of the cholera, and shut off many of the wells and aqueducts that were infected with the bacteria. Additionally, they quarantined Manzanillo, and even canceled Carnival in the city of Bayamo, in order to avoid any more cases of cholera there. We were told by our bike-taxi driver in Bayamo that there was only one case there now, and that it was from someone who came from Manzanillo. However, I am certain that he was misinformed, as it would make no sense to cancel Bayamo's Carnival because of one random case. This suggested that many people were misinformed about the situation, as the government was trying to keep it under wraps in order to not frighten away the tourists. I found out about the outbreak through the news in the United States before leaving for Cuba. Had I not been informed about it before leaving, I would have had no idea about the outbreak.

After taking all of that into consideration, Katie and I decided that we still wanted to go to Bayamo, as it was a place that many people had spoken about highly. Also, I had been looking forward to playing chess in the park with the local *Bayameses* ("people of Bayamo"). Unfortunately, that wish never materialized because I could not find an open table to play anyone. I even tried to walk to the Chess Academy, but they were not open the day I passed by. In any case, Katie only had one day to spend in Bayamo, as she was going to get the night bus from Bayamo to Trinidad, which was a nine-hour overnight bus. So once we got to Bayamo, and were taken to the *casa* by a bike taxi, we set our stuff down and headed out for the town center.

Bayamo was full of history, as it was the city where Carlos Manuel de Céspedes lived, as well as Pedro Felipe Figueredo, the man who wrote the national anthem of the Republic of Cuba. That was a big deal, especially taking into account that Bayamo was not a large city. And I was told that the *Bayameses* were extremely happy to sing it for you in the street. Unfortunately, we didn't have the pleasure of being serenaded in this way while we were running around the city checking out all of the sites before dropping Katie off at the Viazul bus station.

Of course, a mandatory stop while in Bayamo was Céspedes' house, which still stands strong in the middle of the *Parque Céspedes*, a park that bears his name, as do many parks in Cuba. His residence was a lovely colonial Spanish house. As interesting and as beautiful as his home was, what I found most interesting in the house was a handwritten letter by Céspedes to Spain about his son, who was captured and ultimately killed during the War of Independence. The story was, the Spanish captured Céspedes' son and asked for Céspedes to cease fire and essentially give up. Unfortunately for the Spanish, Céspedes was willing to sacrifice his son for the independence of Cuba. In fact, I would presume that his son would have concurred if he were asked, as he was fighting in the war too. Céspedes said that "Oscar is not my only son, I am the father of all the Cubans who have died for Cuba." To me, that was fascinating: to believe in the War of Independence with such conviction that he was willing to sacrifice his own son for the freedom of everyone else. (Hmmm, sounds like another story I have heard of...)

Another memorable part of Bayamo was the *paseo* ("main avenue") that cut through Bayamo, adjacent to the park and Céspedes' house, and ran parallel to *Calle José Martí* (another whose name is honored on streets in every city of Cuba). This *paseo* was filled with artwork, pavers, gazeboes for shade, and interesting restaurants that I hadn't seen anywhere else in Cuba. In my opinion, this *paseo* is one of the most unusual *paseos* in all of Cuba, in terms of artsyness and originality. The only place that I would say rivals Bayamo's *paseo* would be *Havana Vieja*. But that is only because it had been completely restored when it was named a UNESCO World Heritage Site.

The *paseo* in Bayamo was home to a wax museum, an aquarium, and an archeology museum, all within fifty meters of one another. They were all small; nevertheless, they were all full of interesting information about Cuba and its history. I can only speak for the wax museum and the archeology museum, as I never made it to the aquarium. The wax museum had figures of José Martí and Céspedes (of course), Carlos Puebla (the revolution's musician), and numerous other historical figures. They even had a wax figure of Ernest Hemingway, because he spent a good portion of his life living in Cuba. To cap it off, he won the Nobel Prize for Literature in 1954 for his book *The Old Man and the Sea,* which is about a fictional old fisherman, named Santiago, who takes his little skiff out to fish off the northern coast of Cuba for over 80 straight days to no avail. Until, alas, on the eighty-fifth day, he catches the "big one," only to have sharks eat it as he is hauling it in to shore.

After a long day of wandering around Bayamo, my *casa* family and I said good-bye to Katie and saw her off to Trinidad, but not before taking a couple of pictures of the Beatles Culture Center that was near the *casa.* This was a place dedicated to Beatles cover bands and Beatles music. So it came as no surprise that they decided to proudly adorn the entrance with larger-than-life-sized bronze Beatles. Yes, the bronze Fab Four were standing there to greet you at the entrance. While I'm not a real fan, as an anthropologist, I hold a special place in my heart for "Lucy in the Sky with Diamonds" for what it means to the world of anthropology and archaeology. Lucy was the name that was given to the Australopithecus afarensis that was found in Ethiopia and was estimated to have lived 3.2 million years ago. She was the hominid that became widely known as "the missing link." And no matter what side of the fence one may be on with regard to evolution, that was certainly an interesting discovery.

One song that was very famous in Cuba was "Imagine," which was written by John Lennon. In Holguín, there was another Beatles-tribute bar that had the lyrics to the song "Imagine" on the windowpane facing out into the main avenue for all to see, read, and admire. It seems to be an inspiring song, lyrically speaking, for the Cuban people particularly, as well as many others across the globe.

I planned to go back to the Beatles Cultural Center in Bayamo later that evening and listen to some of their music, even though it was going to be recorded, and not live. However, when I went back past the Beatles Cultural Center later that night, all I found was one employee sitting outside, and the place was empty. When I got closer to ask him if it was open, he looked at me and asked me, "What do you want?" And so I answered him with a very logical answer. After all, what would anyone want who was showing up at the front door of a music center that had music in the evenings? I said, "Well, I wanted to go in." Then he told me that it was closed, as there was no one there. I thought to myself, *Of course no one is there, you didn't even turn the music on to attract anyone to the place.* So I just acknowledged the fact that he did not feel like working. After all, he was getting paid the same whether he chose to work or not, so why bother, right? I later found out that the live Beatles cover bands are only on the weekends.

After that relatively awkward experience, I called it a night and made my way back to my *casa* to hang out with my host family, which, to my surprise, turned out to be a late night of sitting on the sidewalk— and on the road—and talking about the differences between the U.S. system and the Cuban system. It was interesting to see how many of the Cuban people were educated and informed, many of them with regard to U.S. politics as well as their own. Given how little access to the outside world they had and were left to rely on the five Cuban channels and the *Granma*, Cuba's most widely read newspaper, it was surprising how well-informed they were. Both the television and the newspaper reported about incidents in the United States. Most of the time, they were pretty accurate.

Our conversation was absorbing, but we stayed up so late talking that I missed my bus to Holguín the next morning and ended up having to wait for the afternoon bus to take me instead. Of course I didn't complain, as it gave me time to sleep in and run some errands, send some e-mails and buy batteries, which were things I needed to take care of anyway. So it all worked out well in the end.

SUPPOSEDLY ANTI-AMERICAN SENTIMENTS

I have heard it said by some Americans who have been to Cuba that they'd never seen so much anti-American propaganda. However, I would have to say that I strongly disagree with this statement, as I have seen more anti-American propaganda in countries in Central and South America than in Cuba. In fact, I would go as far as to say that there was very little propaganda directly targeted at the United States in Cuba. The propaganda that I saw came in the form of billboards and graffiti artwork. Yet, few of these specifically spoke out against the United States. One of the billboards of this type that stuck out to me, however, was the billboard that people see as they leave the airport in Havana. That particular billboard, which I described in the chapter "Welcome to Cuba," was directed at the U.S.-imposed trade embargo that was put in place by John F. Kennedy over fifty years ago. That was not the only signage that spoke out against the United States, as there were a few more scattered across the country. Nonetheless, very little of it was specifically directed at the United States. Perhaps it could be said that *Granma*, Cuba's most popular newspaper, has a tendency to highlight the bad news about the United States. But couldn't it also be said that the United States does the same thing about Cuba and other countries around the world where they want to sway popular opinion about a particular country—North Korea, Venezuela, Iran, and Cuba, just to name a few?

On the other hand, there were a lot of billboards, graffiti, and slogans that promoted Cuba's socialist ideology. This should not be confused with anti-American propaganda. Just because a country's ideology is contrary to the United States' ideology and is being promoted freely within their own country does not mean it should be deemed anti-American rhetoric or propaganda. As I travelled across the entire country, I saw very little anti-U.S. sentiment.

Surprisingly, I didn't even see any anti-American propaganda in and around the province of Guantanamo, which is where the infamous United States Naval base (and terrorist prison) is located. It's true that I spent very little time in Guantanamo, but even so, in that short time, I didn't see anything anti-American. Perhaps, if I were to have gone closer to the base, then maybe I would have seen some sort of anti-American propaganda. Interestingly enough, it has been said that during the height of the Cuban Missile Crisis and subsequent falling-out between the U.S. and Cuba, the area surrounding the U.S. military base at Guantanamo was more heavily mined per square foot by the U.S. than anywhere in Vietnam during the Vietnam War. So one might assume that the Cubans who live around the base are less than pleased with the U.S. presence there.

Even so, I've seen more anti-U.S. rhetoric in countries such as Nicaragua, Honduras, and Argentina. I am highlighting countries who have witnessed the negative repercussions of some of the U.S.-imposed neoliberalist policies, most notably, NAFTA (North American Free Trade Agreement) and CAFTA-DR (Central American Free Trade Agreement - Dominican Republic). These agreements sought to stimulate economic growth in these countries. However, one might argue that these policies have increased the wealth gap between the rich and poor. Cuba, on the other hand, has been immune to these policies as a result of the trade embargo. It seems that it would make little sense to disparage the United States in a country where U.S. citizens are not legally allowed to travel without special permission. Rather, Cuba seemed to focus more attention on promoting the revolution and its ideology than on criticizing the United States of America. In fact, it could be perceived that Cuba is so distracted by promoting its own history so excessively that it has essentially lost sight of anything else.

Even so, this is not to suggest that Cuba was free of political discontent. On the contrary, there is a great deal of unhappiness. For one thing, I would assert that Cuba's government is extremely paranoid, precisely because they were so obsessed with keeping their revolutionary ideology intact. Moreover, one of the things that I found a bit frustrating in Cuba was that it seemed that when I was there, I was cut off from the rest of the world. While most of the time I find this to be a good thing when traveling, in this case, lacking enough infrastructure to have things such as Wi-Fi made widely available made it hard to communicate with the outside world. This makes it difficult for the Cubans to learn about things outside of Cuba. Internet access would make a world of difference with regard to research and learning. The Internet is not, in general, something reserved only for developed countries, as Nicaragua—the second poorest country in the Western Hemisphere—has Wi-Fi in numerous coffee shops, restaurants, and hotels, even in the most remote places.

I was told by a person who works for a Cuban information company that they were currently in the process of building the infrastructure to be able to handle the number of users who would start using the Internet. However, he agreed with me when I raised the question about censorship, and which websites the government would allow to be viewed. I raised that question because I was told that even the doctors in Havana—as well as the people working for the information companies—had to sign in when they used the Internet, and were only allowed to view sites that were pertinent to their work. Close censorship does not lend itself to surfing the Internet, or to free, inventive thought for that matter. Although the Internet is certainly full of false information and distractions, having the freedom to freely research things or surf the Web is certainly something that can lend itself to both personal and educational development.

Additionally, it has been suggested by other Cubans, according to what they were told by the State, that the reason the State hadn't approved countrywide Internet for all Cubans was that they were concerned with the issue of pornography. So naturally, my reply was that "if Internet providers and governments shut down the access of a whole country because of pornography, then no country as a whole would have Internet." I am not suggesting that all people that have the

Internet view, sell, or even condone pornography. However, it is widely known that pornography is a lucrative industry that thrives on the Internet. Still, you cannot shut down access for a whole nation and limit the citizens of a that country from accessing information on the World Wide Web simply because a small percentage of people will be involved in pornography. It is hard to believe that could be the main reason.

It could be considered that the State is concerned about giving Cubans access to the Internet because it would allow them access to *objective* (I am using that word very loosely) information about the world, as well as the good and the bad as it pertains to their own country and its leaders. Perhaps the fear is that the Cuban people would be exposed to, or read about, other ideologies and worldviews. This, in turn, could directly affect, and perhaps, threaten, the current ideology set forth by the revolution and the Cuban government. On close examination, there are only a few justifiable reasons why Cuba would deprive its people of access to the Internet—and foreign travel as well. Naturally, having access to other ideologies, worldviews, and ways of thinking may, perhaps, lead the Cuban people to question their own government, and that could lead to another revolution. I am not saying that this would happen; I am just suggesting this as a legitimate fear for not allowing all Cubans to have access to the Internet.

It should be noted that there was Internet in Cuba, and it's accessible for tourists who could afford to pay $6 an hour to use it. Given that even the highest paid Cuban professionals don't make more than the equivalent of $50–$70 U.S. dollars a month, an hour of Internet would be approximately one-fifth of their monthly earnings. Moreover, locals are not allowed to use the Internet at these Internet cafés even if they hypothetically had $6 for one hour. And if a Cuban resident wanted to have the Internet in his or her home, it was extremely expensive. For example, in Santiago de Cuba, I was told that it would cost over $100 a month for slow Internet access—so slow that people couldn't even open social media sites and e-mail websites outside of the Cuban e-mail system.

This could be attributed to lack of infrastructure; however, if the poorest countries in the Western Hemisphere, like Nicaragua, have the infrastructure to have Wi-Fi and Internet access, then Cuba could at least partner with a Mexican or a Venezuelan company in order to build sound, stable Internet infrastructure in Cuba. It doesn't have to be an American company, so using the embargo as rhetoric to deprive the Cuban people access to the World Wide Web is misplaced. Limiting access to the Internet and monitoring people's activity raises suspicion as to the reason why Cubans aren't allowed full access to the Internet. The concern about pornography doesn't seem to be a strong argument.

This brings me to the next point, which has to do with the low salaries here in Cuba. It could be argued that Cuba is falling victim to what I have referred to as a massive domestic brain drain, as many of the professionals are going to continue to make a move toward the tourism industry and leave their professions. This, in turn, would be detrimental to the revolution's ideology, the high level of education among Cubans, and ultimately the Cuban socialist model as a whole. The heart of the Cuban society is the working professionals. They are the ones who pay the taxes, and therefore sustain their socialist system.

Consequently, if people begin to leave their professional careers to work in the tourism industry, then Cuba will end up without good doctors, teachers, nurses, and so on, because everyone will be taxi drivers, *jineteras* (prostitutes), or *casa particular* owners. One of the major reasons that Cuba is unable to pay their professionals a higher wage is because the current socialist system that is in place is responsible for paying these individuals, as well as providing for the rest of the country's citizens. They use taxes to guarantee all Cubans food, free education, and free health care, among other things. It has been said that Cuba is the only place in the world where you can live well and never work, because the State will take care of you. That, typically, doesn't lend itself to a competitive society, because a significant number of its citizens will live primarily on government handouts. Meanwhile, those that want to work and get ahead will be held back by the government, as competition, in the eyes of the current Cuban government, is seen as one of the ugly faces of capitalism.

Another unfortunate truth about the State-paid professionals is that they are paid in Cuban pesos, which is a currency that isn't even valued in their own country. Most people would rather have CUCs, as the CUC is pegged against the dollar, the euro, and other internationally respected currencies. So while Cuban professionals are being paid in national pesos, the Cubans who work in the tourism industry are being paid in CUCs. In fact, when I was in an Internet *café* in Holguín, I tried to pay the person working there in Cuban pesos, and she told me that I could only pay in CUC, as Cuban pesos are, as she put it, "worthless here." I reminded her that the Cuban peso was the currency of Cuba. But instead of getting into an argument about how sad it was that their own currency wasn't accepted even in their own county, and how challenging it must be for a State employee like this individual to survive on Cuban pesos, I just paid in CUCs and walked out. That type of disrespect toward their own currency raises the question as to how the Cuban state expects professionals to get ahead, or even make ends meet. I am confident that the government officials are not struggling in that way. It would only be logical that they are the ones who are so adamant about perpetuating the Cuban socialist system exactly as it is.

Let me reiterate that it's not the socialist ideology itself that is to blame for the lack of social reforms; rather, it is Cuba's lack of infrastructure and low GDP (60.81 billion USD), combined with excessive limitations on freedom of speech and expression, that has seemingly created a system that not only does not reward hard work, but also doesn't allow free thought to manifest itself in such a way as to offer the Cuban people a sense of true freedom that is fruitful and beneficial for the entire society. Thus, it puts a strain on social and economic development. Again, it is hard to blame Cuba entirely, as the embargo that has been placed on them for over fifty years has played a large role in this lack of development. Even so, the embargo is not new, and by now they should have found ways to foster more economic and intellectual development.

The Cuban socialist mindset, in theory, is fine; however, Cuba has no money to successfully support its ideology, and therefore fails to compensate its professionals with adequate salaries. Ultimately that has led to an domestic brain drain, as has been discussed in previous chapters. And even though it would be easy to blame all of this on the embargo, Cuba has been so determined to keep this ideology in place and intact that it has made it hard to partner with any of the world's superpowers to increase their economic potential. Of course Cuba was living well when they were being heavily funded by the Soviet Union. Unfortunately, those days are long gone, and now Cuba needs to partner with a country that will help them maximize their potential as a beautiful Caribbean island. It should be noted that in recent years there seemed to be an international partnership starting up between the emerging world superpower, China, and Cuba. Only time will tell how that partnership will play out. Perhaps it will prove to be the catalyst that Cuba needs in order to restructure its socialist system and get back on track. China, while remaining a communist country, has enacted many reforms to its economy to facilitate its development and growth. A strong partnership with a like-minded superpower may be precisely what Cuba needs to continue to perpetuate its socialist revolution.

CONCLUDING THOUGHTS

It is always such a bittersweet feeling when all of my shampoo, toothpaste, and the other things that I have brought on my trip with me start to come to an end. It's bittersweet because it reminds me that my trip is almost over; however, the beautiful thing is that I know that after a long stint of traveling, I will walk away with new insights into another culture, another perspective, and another world, which, in sum total, is one of the greatest gifts traveling can offer anyone. As my trip came to a close, I was confronted with the inevitable question from my Cuban friends, "What do you think about Cuba?" And even though that had been a relatively easy question for me to answer after my first trip to Cuba, this time just saying "It's amazing" didn't truly articulate how I felt about it. Cuba is much too complicated of a country to give it a simple and reactive answer like, "It's amazing."

Cuba was without question one of the most beautiful places that I have visited in Latin America, in terms of its landscapes, its history, and its people. Socially, culturally, and physically, it is without a doubt one of the most extraordinary places that I have been to in Latin America. Furthermore, it is quite possibly one of the last socialist strongholds remaining in the world, an accomplishment that has certainly come with its struggles—not just financially, but also politically, with threats and attempts to topple Fidel and his government. It has been said that Fidel has had more than six hundred assassination attempts made on his life over the past fifty-plus years. So it has been an uphill battle right from the start to keep their socialist ideology in place. This ideology has inspired other Latin American countries such as Venezuela, Ecuador, Nicaragua, and Bolivia, to follow in the footsteps of "the Maximum Leader," Fidel Castro.

Returning to the question that I was asked by my friends regarding my opinion of Cuba, I have to admit that if I were to have been asked this question after my first trip, I would have naively said that Cuba is amazing, the system is working extremely well, and the Cuban people are, by and large, happy people under the Castro government. A little more experience has made this a little more debatable, and up for interpretation. It is extremely challenging to get an objective answer without experiencing these things for oneself. It requires a person to sift through a lot of rhetoric and propaganda, on both sides of the sociopolitical spectrum.

I want to be clear that I am not saying that Cuba should adopt the United States' ideology. Quite the contrary, there are only a few changes that I would consider making in Cuba if I were the successor to Castro.

Those changes would be, without a doubt, a higher acceptance of freedom of speech and freedom of expression, which could permit critiquing the government in a nonviolent way. Another thing that I think should change are the salaries and the dual monetary system that is used in Cuba, because to a certain degree, it segregates the Cubans from the tourists and tourist-industry providers, since the Cubans use national pesos and the tourists use convertible pesos. These two currencies have created two classes divided by their monetary systems, which among its other drawbacks, is not very socialist. Furthermore, it has inserted this class distinction between the Cubans who work for *el Estado*, and those who are involved in the tourism industry. Not to mention the damage done by the fact that those who work in the tourism industry make more than the people who work for the State, including doctors, nurses, teachers, engineers, and other professionals. Those who work for the State spend years earning their degree, and are also the ones who sustain the revolutionary ideology. So it doesn't seem fair that those people are paid a mere $20–$50 a month while the people who drive a private taxi, for example, earn a significantly higher salary.

In terms of the class dichotomy, I feel that raising the salaries of those who work for the State would encourage more people to continue studying and pursuing a career that pays back into the real Cuban economy, instead of trying to make money from the tourists who come to Cuba. Because the salaries are so low, the temptation to get involved with tourist-based work is that much more enticing. Thus, if the salaries that were paid by the State were more competitive, then there would be fewer people leaving the true Cuban economy—a process I described earlier as an domestic brain drain). With all that said, Cuba can still boast that they have one doctor for approximately every 170 Cuban citizens, an achievement that is hard to beat even in the most developed countries. This doesn't even take into account the Cuban doctors who are working abroad doing their medical missions in eighty-three countries across the world. Yet they still earn very little in comparison to doctors who work in developed regions like the United States and Western Europe. The eighty-three countries where these exported doctors work are mostly in the developing south.

The third change that should be made would be to allow Cubans to travel and have full access to the Internet. In other words, offer the Cuban people, not only doctors or a select few professionals, the freedom to travel outside of the country and surf the World Wide Web. Something that the Cuban people long to do, according to what I was told, is to travel. All of the Cubans who confided this to me also said that they didn't want to travel so that they could leave Cuba; rather, they simply wanted to see other parts of the world just like other people do. It must be pretty difficult for the Cuban people to see tourists come to Cuba, travel around, enjoy the beauties of the Cuban culture, and then return home. That seemed to be a constant complaint among the Cuban people with whom I spoke.

In short, free speech would allow for better personal development. Raising salaries would allow Cubans to save their money and have a disposable income to put back into the economy. And allowing them the opportunity to travel would give them a chance to see the world and learn about other cultures and ways of life. This will only enrich the Cuban people's understanding of the world around them and allow them to grow and develop as free human beings. It could even give them a greater appreciation of Cuba, with its free education, low-cost housing, and other social benefits. This would ultimately benefit Cuba.

Let me reiterate something pertaining to one of the three changes that I mentioned: I think that in order to continue perpetuating the socialist ideology of the revolution, the State should consider raising the salaries of the professionals in Cuba. The only problem is that Cuba has a relatively low GDP because it has very few natural resources, and therefore, it exports very little outside of Cuba. One example of an export would be nickel, which is something that is exported to places such as Canada. Still, outside of a few potential exports like sugar, and maybe cigars, there are very few natural resources in Cuba. Thus, the option of exporting goods and services outside of Cuba is relatively bleak. In fact, I suspect that most of Cuba's GDP is earned from tourism. And even though Cuba is a world-class tourist destination, tourism alone is not sufficient to support and sustain its 12,000,000 citizens. What Cuba has managed to do with so few natural resources and a low GDP is impressive, because it offers all of its citizens access to free health care, free education, and a monthly ration of food, among other things.

Furthermore, Cuba, with its current governmental and economic system, has managed to resist the current imperialist powers that have long sought to flex their imperialist, hegemonic muscles over this island nation with the intention of making it surrender to a capitalist agenda. Only time will tell if Cuba can continue to promote and perpetuate the revolution's ideology and survive as its own, unaltered, independent nation, whose ideology is contrary to the leaders of most countries across the globe.

Taking all of that into consideration, I would still say that I genuinely like Cuba, and that it is one of the most fascinating countries that I have ever visited. This is taking into account its indigenous history, its beautiful beaches, rivers, countryside, waterfalls, and its people, as well as the current sociopolitical system and political history with the United States, the Soviet Union, and the world in general. Regarding Cuba's international impact, it is interesting to note that Cuba has sent troops to support other leftist liberation movements in Latin America, such as Grenada, Nicaragua and El Salvador, in the

Congo, Ethiopia, and Angola, as well as Vietnam, supporting the North Vietnamese. In addition, Cuba currently has doctors serving on medical missions in eighty-three countries around the world. So speaking as a Latin American anthropologist, Cuba is impressive. And speaking as a tourist, Cuba is, in my opinion, the unpolished gem of the Caribbean. I believe that once the trade embargo is lifted, then the American people will come and see all of this for themselves.

On the other hand, coming back for a second time allowed me to dive deeper into the culture in order to see things from a different perspective—one that ultimately opened my eyes to some of the less favorable realities of the Cuban system. Of course, no country and no political or economic system is perfect, so this is not discrediting Cuba as the only country with political or economic flaws. However, during my second trip, I became aware of some of the painful realities that the Cuban people have had to endure as a result of the current political system. These were realities that were not as apparent to me during my first trip. Perhaps one could sense naiveté in the early chapters of this book.

During my second trip, I had the chance to see Cuba in greater detail, as I spent more time in fewer places, allowing me a more in-depth view. The bulk of my trip was spent in Baracoa and Holguín, which allowed me to learn more about the day-to-day lives of the Cuban people in these areas. On my first trip to Cuba, I was only able to spend three to four days in each city. That was done intentionally because I wanted to cover more ground, and see and learn as much as possible. However, for the second trip, I was afforded the luxury of taking a step back in order to observe things less from the perspective of a tourist, and more from the perspective of a Cuban.

That being said, I am still a tourist nonetheless. And being a tourist has both afforded me luxuries that many Cubans will never see, even in their own country, as well as having prevented me from going further into the culture, where the government and the local revolutionary committees have made it clear that certain things are off-limits for tourists.

Nevertheless, in my analysis of Cuba, I made every effort to do away with any and all preconceived judgments or prejudices in my mind, in order not to be overly critical of Cuba without first researching things firsthand as objectively as possible. However, at the risk of comparing the two countries, it must be said that one of the major differences between the United States and Cuba is that, in the United States, one can openly and nonviolently critique the system without having to look over one's shoulder for fear of being denounced and subsequently imprisoned for being "anti-revolutionary." And even though I noticed some of this paranoia on my first trip, it wasn't as obvious to me as it was on my second trip. Even the *casa* owners don't tend to open up to you as much as they would like until you see it with your own eyes. And at that point, there is no need for words.

As I was reflecting on my trip across Cuba, I was reminded of a conversation that I had with a Cuban friend of mine when I was in Honduras shortly after my first trip to Cuba. He said that in Cuba, it's too hard to get ahead because of the system. I answered that at least all Cubans have an opportunity to study, to eat, and so on, and that those things are luxuries in most of the developing world. And even though he couldn't argue with the fact that all Cubans have access to a proper education, doctors, food, and a home—which is generally passed down from the previous generation—he said that the Cuban people are not rewarded for working hard. He also said that the only reason he has been successful in Honduras is because he has worked hard. He also insinuated that if you work hard in countries like Honduras, then anyone can get ahead. I respectfully told him that he was totally mistaken, but not in an argumentative way.

I said that the reason for his success in Honduras could, in all likelihood, be attributed to three things, two of which most Hondurans will never have access to: hard work, a good education, which teaches you how to learn, and opportunity. I then added that yes, he did work hard; however, without an education provided to him by the Cuban socialist system, and an opportunity where he could use his education and apply his hard work, then he would just be another hard-working poor person in a developing country like Honduras. I have only one friend out of all of my hundreds of friends in Honduras that has improved his life because of hard work. In most cases, hard-working people work for only about $300 a month all across Latin America. That is why they risk their lives to come to the United States. It is not because the U.S. culture is so amazing, but for the perceived hope that there will be an opportunity to make a better future. In short, I told my Cuban friend that he has been able to become successful in Honduras not simply because of hard work, but rather because of the education he has and the opportunity he was given. And after a long discourse about the Cuban system, he and I eventually saw eye to eye.

As a last thought, I think that it would be appropriate to add the thought that if Che were alive and had been able to mold Cuba into the country he envisioned, Cuba might look very different. In the book *Philosophical and Political Ideologue* (*Idearío Político y Filosófico del Che*, Che Guevara, Editora Política, 1991), he continually referred to a Cuba that was free of classes, or at least a ruling class, saying that Cuba was to be run by the proletariat, or working-class Cubans. That is not the situation in modern-day Cuba, as Cuba is filled with committees and governmental sycophants. But then again, what government isn't? Making an assertion that Cuba would be different if Che Guevara were still alive is merely speculation, and perhaps a bit idealistic, as there is absolutely no way to substantiate such a claim.

In the end, one of the most important things that I took away from this adventure were the memories of the beautiful places that I had the privilege to see and all of the wonderful people that I met, and who welcomed me into their lives. Still, if I were asked my opinion about Cuba's political and economic system itself, it would be an extremely tough question to answer. Cuba is unique in terms of its sociopolitical ideology, and for someone like me, who grew up in a totally different system, it is something that I will need to contemplate and digest for a long time. There are so many things that this country offers to its citizens that other countries cannot or do not: free education, free health care, food, and housing assistance. All of these rights are amazing, and it could certainly be argued that from a theoretical perspective, Cuba's ideology is great; however, how it plays out in realistic and practical terms continues to be an extremely polemical debate.

I hope that these chapters have served to at least shed a bit of light on the good, the bad, and the ugly of Cuba behind the embargo. There are so many remarkable things that the Cuban culture has to offer their people, as well as their tourists; still, Cuba, just like any other country across the world, is not perfect. No country is. And Cuba, I have been told, is in the process of reassessing their current situation in order to raise the standard of living of their citizens by allowing them more freedom to own private businesses, which will begin to open the doors to more capitalist endeavors.

Naturally, there is much speculation about the effects that capitalism will have on the socialist system, given that capitalism has long been considered Cuba's economic nemesis. It will inevitably bring about a change to Cuba's ideology and future. Whether or not that is a good or bad thing at this point remains to be seen.

The Cuban spirit and capacity to survive against all odds is a testament to the Cuban character—a character that is built to endure and persevere, but at the same time, full of an inexplicable *joie de vivre*. I can say with certainty that if I were to have the opportunity to return, to show my friends this beautiful island, and to introduce them to the people that I met during my time in Cuba, I would be honored to visit this intriguing island nation again. It is a place that has earned a special place in my heart, not just for all of the amazing things, but also for the not-so-amazing things. Because that is what makes Cuba the country it is, and sets her apart from the rest of the world. And in conclusion, I think that it would be appropriate to evoke the famous words of Che Guevara, who, in 1964, at the United Nations, ended a famous speech about the new Cuban government and his dedication to keeping the Cuban Revolution's ideology alive at all costs: *"Patria o muerte!"*[33]

APPENDIX

Legend
Major Cities Mentioned
Provinces
Topographic Layout
Value
High : 1736
Low : -7
Viñales
La Habana
Varadero
Playa Girón
Cienfuegos
Santa Clara
Trinidad
Camagüey
Manzanillo
Holguín
Bayamo
Gibara
Santiago de Cuba
Guantánamo
Moa
N
Source: DivaGIS
Author: Jesse Casanova

PHOTOS

Parque Céspedes, Bayamo, Cuba

Billboard in Birán, Cuba

Book vendor in Old Havana

Che Guevara's mausoleum in Santa Clara, Cuba

Taxi in Old Havana

El Yunque National Park in Baracoa, Cuba

Ministry of Industry Building in the
Plaza de la Revolución, in Havana, Cuba

La Bodeguita del Medio in Old Havana,
haunt of such luminaries as Salvadore Allende, Pablo Neruda, Victor
Hugo, Ernest Hemingway, and others

The Moncada Barracks in Santiago de Cuba, which Fidel Castro
and his forces attacked on July 26, 1953

Che Guevara prints for sale in Havana, Cuba

Pork sandwiches in Gibara, Cuba, during Carnival

View of Havana, Cuba, from the other side
of the Bay of Havana

Guardalavaca Beach in Holguín

Colonial streets of Trinidad, Cuba

Statue of José Martí in Old Havana
near the Capitol Building

GLOSSARY

Anthrotourism
A form of travel where the goal is to consciously integrate into the cultural framework of the society in which you are traveling and living.

el Apostle
The Apostle, a title used for José Martí

(la) Avenida
Avenue

(el) Bici-taxi
A bicycle taxi

el Bloqueo
The Embargo

Bahía de Cochinos
Bay of Pigs

La Bahía de Havana
The Bay of Havana

Bayameses
The people of Bayamo

(el) Cacique
Spanish word derived from the Taino, meaning a chieftain

Café americano
Brewed coffee

Café cubano
Espresso with sugar

(la) Caldosa
Stew

Campesino
Someone who lives and works in *el campo*, or countryside

La Canasta Básica (CBA)
Literally, "the basic basket," this term refers to the monthly food allowance given to each Cuban. See note 18.

Casa
House

La Casa de la Música
Literally, "House of Music," a chain of nightclubs in Havana and around Cuba

La Casa de la Trova
Literally, "House of the Trova," another nightclub chain. "Trova" is a traditional folk music genre in Cuba.

Casa Particular
Literally, "private house"; See note 16.

Castillo de los Tres Reyes del Morro
Castle of the Three Kings, named after the three Magi in the Bible. The "Morro" is the name for the headland or rock at the entrance to Havana's harbor, which is where the Castle is located.

el Centro
The "center," or downtown area

(el) Chavito
The Cuban convertible peso, which is the tourist currency also known as the CUC

Comités de Defensa de la Revolución
Committees for the Defense of the Revolution, or CDR, an organization established to monitor the local community

Compañeros
Companions

el Cuartel Moncada
The Moncada Barracks, located in Santiago de Cuba

(la) Cuenta
The check or bill (as at a restaurant)

La Cueva del Agua
The Cave of Water, located in Baracoa

(la) Cueva de las Golondrinas
Cave of the Golondrinas (a type of bird), located in Viñales; See *golandrina*.

La Cueva de Paraíso
The Cave of Paradise, located in Baracoa

Las Damas de Blanco
The Women in White. These women march in Havana as a form of nonviolent protest against the Castro administration.

Developing south
A geographical description for the countries in Latin America, Africa, and Asia that are underdeveloped.

el Estado
Literally, "the state," meaning the government

Estadounidense
Literally, "statesman," this is a term for citizens of the United States of America. Though all people who live in the Americas are *Americano*, the Spanish-speaking world refers to people from the United States as *"Americanos."*

Golondrina
A swallow (avian)

Gracias
Thank you

La Gran Piedra
Literally, "the Big Rock," located in Santiago de Cuba

Granma
1. Literally, "grandmother," the name of the boat that was taken by Fidel and Che's men from the coast of Mexico to Cuba;
2. Cuba's most widely-read newspaper, named for the boat

Gringo
American (or Canadian)

(la) Guagua
Bus

(la) Guyabera
A typical Cuban man's shirt

(la) Hacienda
Plantation

Havana Vieja
Literally, "Old Havana"

Holguinero
Someone who is from Holguín, Cuba

El Hotel Nacional
The National (State-run) Hotel

(el) jeepe
A jeep (pronounced jeep-eh)

El Jefe
Literally, "the Boss," applied to Raphael Trujillo; See note 20.

Lindo
Good-looking

Jineteras
Prostitutes; escorts. *Jineteros* are male escorts.

(la) Loma
Hill

La Loma de la Cruz
The Hill of the Cross (in Holguín)

Malecón
Boardwalk, or esplanade. In Havana, the malecón is a bulkhead that runs the length of Havana's coastline.

(el) Mochilero
Backpacker

(el) Movimiento 26 de Julio
The name and date associated with the Cuban Revolution. On July 26, 1953, the first attempt at a revolution was launched: an attack on the Moncada Barracks in Santiago de Cuba.

Museo de la Lucha Clandestina
Museum of the Clandestine Fight, located in Santiago de Cuba

Museo de la Revolución
Museum of the Revolution, located in Havana

The New Man
The idea, promulgated by Che Guevara, that people are willing to work, not only for themselves, but also for the betterment of the society in which they live.

Nos vemos ahí
See you in heaven

Operation Condor
Operation by U.S. intelligence agencies to support right-wing dictatorships in Central and South America, initiated in 1975

El Oriente
Literally, "the East," or the far eastern part of the island of Cuba

(el) Paladar
A privately-run restaurant

(la) Palapa
An open-sided beach hut with a thatched roof, or any shelter on the beach

Papá
Dad, or father

Pargo
Snapper (the fish)

Particular
Private, as in a private enterprise

El Parque de los Amigos
The Park of the Friends, located in Ybor City in Tampa, Florida

(el) paseo
Main avenue

Patente
Patent, or the right to own a private business such as a *casa particular*

"...pioneros por el comunismo. Seremos como El Che"
"...pioneers of communism. We will be like Che," from the Cuban Pledge of Allegiance, said in schools just as in the U.S.

Patria o muerte
Literally, "Homeland or death." See note 33.

La Playa del Este
Literally, "Eastern Beach"

Remesas
Remittances, often sent from Cuban-American U.S. residents to their families still living in Cuba

Las Romerias de Mayo
The May Pilgrimages

Santeria
A blend of Catholicism and African traditions that began to emerge after the arrival of the African slaves at the beginning of the 16th century

Sí
Yes

Si Eu Te Pego
Portuguese song title meaning "Oh, If I Catch You"

Sin azúcar
Without sugar

The Special Period
A period of time which started in 1991, following the collapse of the USSR. During that time, without the support

of the Soviet Union, Cuba went into an economic freefall, and people had to ration everything carefully.

(el) Suerte de principiante
Beginner's luck

Tapas
Appetizers

Te quiero
Literally, "I want you," translates to "Love ya!"

(la) terraza
Terrace

(la) Tienda
The store

El Tren Blindado
Literally, "the Bulletproof Train," referring to the train that carried Batista's soldiers to their final stand against the revolutionaries on December 31, 1958. The train was derailed by Che and his men, leading to the surrender of the troops in this confrontation, and, ultimately, the war.

La Universidad de Habana
The University of Havana

(la) Vida nocturna
Nightlife

Washington Consensus
A term originally outlining some specific approaches to assisting developing nations in crisis, the term now refers to an approach oriented towards a strongly market-based solutions system. Also known as "neoliberalism" or "market fundamentalism."

El Yunque
Literally, "the Anvil," a national park named for the anvil-shaped rock that rises above it

NOTES

1   Here is what Humberto Fontova, son of Cuban refugees who left briefly after the Cuban Revolution, has to say about this infamous image in his book *Exposing the Real Che Guevara*: "Much credit for the remarkable afterlife of Che Guevara goes, of course, to The Picture. To his credit, Guevara understood his role. He performed magnificently at his photo shoot in March 1960 for Alberto Korda. His 'faraway' eyes and his high cheekbones were perfectly highlighted…Few Americans know that the famous icon photo was actually spiked by the Castro regime when it was first scheduled to run in Cuba's official paper, *Revolución*. Che's image could have overshadowed the Maximum Leader's at the time…" (Umberto Fontova, *Exposing the Real Che Guevara*; Sentinel, 2008, Introduction, p. xxviii)

"Seven years after Korda's photo shoot, when Che was safely 'sleeping with the fishes' and could pose no threat to the Maximum Leader, Castro dusted off The Picture and started plastering it all over Cuba. He called the international media with a sharp whistle and said, fetch. The result is the most reproduced and idolized print of the century. His former comrades could have told you, 'Fidel Castro only praises the dead.'" (Fontova, xxix)

2   The dictionary definition of Marxism-Leninism is that it is a far-left ideology based on principles of class conflict, egalitarianism, dialectical materialism, rationalism, and social progress. It is anti-bourgeois, anti-capitalist, anti-conservative, anti-fascist, anti-imperialist, anti-liberal, anti-reactionary, and is opposed to bourgeois democracy. It also shifts the paradigm away from simply looking internally at a country and begins to shift the focus towards developing world versus developed world. In other words, it seeks to identify the world's imperial

powers and assign blame to them for their colonization of the world's developing nations.

3   Che Guevara was given the nickname Che by his Cuban friends because he used that word so much. "Che" is a common word used by Argentines that is similar to the slang term of endearment "Dude" in English.

4   John Fitzgerald Kennedy, often referred to by his initials JFK, was the thirty-fifth president of the United States, serving from 1961 until his assassination in 1963. He was the president who was responsible for launching the U.S.-backed Bay of Pigs Invasion in 1961, as well as imposing the trade embargo on Cuba in 1962.

5   The United States embargo against Cuba (also known as, *el bloqueo*, or "the blockade" in English) is a commercial, economic, and financial embargo partially imposed on Cuba in October 1960, shortly after the triumph of the Cuban Revolution, after Cuba nationalized the properties of United States citizens and corporations. The total worth of nationalized property totaled over $500 million in losses to these companies and individuals. In 1962, the embargo was strengthened to a full embargo on Cuba. Currently, the embargo is said to be one of the longest-standing embargos against another country in modern history.

6   At this point, post-World War II, the United States and the Soviet Union (USSR) had emerged as the world's two largest superpowers. Even though Truman initially told Winston Churchill to leave the Turks and the Soviets alone to "figure matters out themselves," it seems that there was a change of heart, and the United States decided to get involved once the Soviets invaded Turkey. In fact, the Soviets continued their occupation of Turkey throughout the mid-1950s. As a result, the United States deployed fifteen nuclear-tipped Jupiter missiles in Turkey on June 1, 1961, which were aimed directly at the Soviet Union.

7   Nikita Sergeyevich Khrushchev was the president of the Soviet Union during the Cuban Missile Crisis and part of the Cold

War. He served as first Secretary of the Communist Party of the Soviet Union from 1953 to 1964, and as Chairman of the Council of Ministers from 1958 to 1964.

8   "The crisis, and its resolution, also shook the foundations of Cuba's developing relationship with the Soviet Union. Khrushchev's decision to withdraw the missiles was made without any consultation with the Cubans, who felt that once again, their sovereignty was being made hostage to great power politics." (Aviva Chomsky, *A History of the Cuban Revolution*; Wiley-Blackwell, 2010, p. 84)

9   This was challenging, as I had to rid myself of all preconceived notions of Cuba, propaganda against Cuba, and anything else that would prevent me from seeing Cuba, its systems, and its people in an objective way.

10 Ernesto Guevara de la Serna y Lynch was born in Rosario, Argentina, on June 14, 1928.

11 President Barack Obama has loosened the restrictions on travel to Cuba as well as sending remittances for Cuban-Americans. Additionally, this has also made it a bit easier for Americans to go to Cuba for academic or missionary purposes.

12 This doesn't mean that they necessarily agreed with Batista *per se*; however, they may have been indifferent to the revolution. Unfortunately, in the eyes of the Fidel Castro and the revolutionary forces, this was seen as insubordination, or subversive behavior, against the revolution.

13 Anthrotourist is a term referring to a person who makes the conscious effort to integrate and understand the cultural framework in which he or she is traveling, as opposed to visiting a country for the purpose of sightseeing or relaxing on the beach. This term comes from my book *Anthrotourist: An Improvised Journey through Latin America* that was published in 2011.

14 Since writing this, the travel situation has changed considerably. In 2012, when I visited, restrictions on U.S. citizens traveling to Cuba were still in effect. See note 11.

15 Technically, the proper term for someone from the United States is *Estadounidense,* which loosely translates to "Statesman." However, even though all people who live in the Americas are *Americano,* the Spanish-speaking world refers to people from the United States as *"Americanos."* It has just become accepted by everyone as the way to refer to someone who is from the United States. Perhaps it is because we call ourselves Americans in English, which is also a misnomer, as all people from the Americas are technically Americans. We just have nothing else to call ourselves when addressing our nationality.

16 The *casa particular* is a privately owned house where the owners convert their house (or a portion thereof) into a place that is suitable for hosting tourists. They determine how many rooms they want to make available to tourists and then they get a *patente* (or patent) from Cuban Immigration. Additionally, as the owner of a *casa particular,* you are responsible for paying taxes to the government every month. The tax is contingent upon how many rooms you have available for tourists and upon your location. For example, in Havana, it costs approximately 150 CUC ($150 USD) per room you make available. The owners of the house are responsible for paying taxes for that patent every month, whether they have guests or not. So it is in their best interest, with regard to occupancy, that Immigration imposes these types of strict laws and penalties for people who try to stay outside of designated tourist housing.

This is an example of a privately owned business in Cuba and is one of a number of capitalist endeavors and changes that the country has undertaken in the recent past (most notably, after the Special Period that almost brought Cuba to its knees, starting in 1991 after the fall of the Soviet Union).

17 This is actually a bit misleading, as I discovered that two of the channels are virtually the same channel.

18 *La Canasta Básica* (CBA) is a monthly ration of food that the Cuban government guarantees to all 12,000,000 Cubans. Included in the *Canasta Básica* are milk, meat, cereal, sugar,

vegetables, fruit, rice, beans, eggs, oil, soap, and toothpaste, among other essential items (like coffee, which, of course, is among the most necessary). For example, for each member of the house, a household is guaranteed 5 lbs. of rice per month. So just to give you an idea of what that looks like on a national scale (just in rice alone), the Cuban government is responsible for providing its citizens, whether they work or not, with 60,000,000 lbs. of rice per month. This is only rice and does not include the eggs and other essential items for survival that the Cuba government supplies its people with on a monthly basis.

19   There is no such thing as professional athletics in Cuba. Therefore, a professional-level baseball player makes between $100–150 a month. In other words, they are not paid exorbitant amounts of money like they are in the United States or even in Europe. It is seen more as a vocation and/or something you do because you enjoy it and is not done for the money.

20   Rafael Trujillo, nicknamed, *El Jefe,* dictator of the Dominican Republic, was quite possibly one of the most brutal dictators in Latin America over the last one hundred years. This is a pretty bold claim considering all of the bloodthirsty dictators that Latin America has witnessed over the last one hundred years. Certainly Fulgencio Batista and Augusto Pinochet, among others, are great candidates for this title. For more information about Trujillo's brutality, read the book *In the Time of the Butterflies* (Julia Alvarez, Algonquin Books, 2010) and look up information about the Parsley Massacres. His misogynistic attitude towards women and his overt racism towards the Haitians living in the border towns around the Dominican Republic and Haitian border are the main topics of these previously mentioned books and themes.

21   Here is the interesting thing with prescriptions. I cannot confirm that they are 100% free; however, in most cases, they are affordable for everyone. The only issue is that while a good majority of the medicines are accessible and inexpensive (essentially the equivalent of what someone with health

insurance and a very low co-pay would pay in the U.S., there are some medicines that are not affordable for people who only operate in the Cuban Peso currency. For example, a woman I met in Trinidad only had the money to buy the basic medication for her leg blood circulation issue because the better medications—the ones she *really* needed—were out of her budget because they were in CUC prices, which made it very expensive for her. In that case, the meds would be like someone with no insurance in the U.S. trying to pay for an expensive prescription while only making minimum wage.

22 There was a point after the revolution when Cuba considered itself a Marxist-Leninist state and at that point in its history, there was certainly a lack of freedom of religion, as people who participated in organized religion were persecuted. It wasn't until the mid-1990s, when Pope John Paul II made a trip to Cuba, that Cuba truly began to open itself up to formal, organized religion. Today, all Cubans are free to worship and be part of organized religion, which was not always the case here in Cuba.

23 *Jineteras*, in Cuba, are women who work as prostitutes within the Cuban society.

24 Camaguey is part of the Ciego de Avila province; however, Trinidad is part of Sancti Spiritus, a province that is adjacent to, and borders, the Ciego de Avila province.

25 These medical missions are not to be confused with a medical mission done by a religious organization. Although these doctors may be affiliated with an organized religion on a personal level, the purpose of these medical mission trips is specifically to do medical work and has nothing to do with sharing their faith with anyone.

26 Some recent United Nations statistics have shown that the gap between the rich and poor has actually increased across Latin American in the countries that have partnered with the United States and their economic ideologies and policies, such as NAFTA (North American Free Trade Agreement) and

CAFTA-DR (Central American Free Trade Agreement and Dominican Republic). However, what is ironic about these statistics is that these policies were created as a way to stimulate economic growth and to decrease the growing gap between rich and poor.

27 Cuban doctors historically have been known for being well respected in their field. Even so, the problem that Cuba faces is that they suffer from lack of funding to maintain the hospitals and to buy medical materials and equipment. For example, I was told by a friend of mine, who did an internship in a hospital in Havana, that the hospital was equipped with CT scanners and other expensive medical equipment; however, her hall went an entire workweek without soap to wash their hands. The subsequent week, they were without running water. The surgeons had to pour rubbing alcohol on their hands before they did any medical procedures, including major surgeries.

28 The most interesting irony to the Kennedy-Castro relationship is that in October of 1963, Kennedy allegedly asked journalist Jean Daniels to publish the following quote in an article in the *New Republic*: "I believe that there is no country in the world including any and all the countries under colonial domination, where economic colonization, humiliation and exploitation were worse than in Cuba, in part owing to my country's policies during the Batista regime. I approved the proclamation which Fidel Castro made in the Sierra Maestra, when he justifiably called for justice and especially yearned to rid Cuba of corruption. I will even go further: to some extent it is as though Batista was the incarnation of a number of sins on the part of the United States. Now we shall have to pay for those sins. In the matter of the Batista regime, I am in agreement with the first Cuban Revolutionaries. That is perfectly clear."

29 It has been said that weeks before Batista died on August 6, 1973, in Marbella, Spain, Fidel had sent assassins there to kill him; however, Batista died of a heart attack before these men could personally do Fidel's dirty work.

30 See *History Will Absolve Me*, Fidel Castro, 1958.

31 From the song "Chan Chan" by The Buena Vista Social Club.

32 This isn't much different than other places across the world; however, it is enforced much more heavily in Cuba as compared to other tourist destinations. At the same time, this heightened level of security is what makes Cuba one of the safest places in the world for both tourists as well as Cubans.

33 This is how Che Guevara ended his speech at the United Nations in 1964 when referring to the determination of the Cuban people to see the revolution succeed as well as their plans for the future of Cuba. The full quote is "¡Patria o Muerte, Venceremos!" which means, "Homeland or death, we shall overcome!" This remains Cuba's motto to this day.

67802935R00128

Made in the USA
Charleston, SC
21 February 2017